IT WORKS

IT WORKS
HOW AND WHY

The Twelve Steps
and Twelve Traditions
of Narcotics Anonymous

Narcotics Anonymous World Services, Inc.
Chatsworth, California

The Twelve Steps and Twelve Traditions reprinted
for adaptation by permission of
AA World Services, Inc.

World Service Office
PO Box 9999
Van Nuys, CA 91409
Tel. (818) 773-9999
Fax (818) 700-0700
Website: www.na.org

World Service Office–EUROPE
Brussels, Belgium
Tel. +32/2/646-6012

World Service Office–CANADA
Mississauga, Ontario

World Service Office–IRAN
Tehran, Iran
www.na-iran.org

Printed in China
17   16   15   33   32

This is NA Fellowship-approved literature.

ISBN 978-1-55776-255-9   English   3/15

WSO Catalog Item No. EN-1143

Table of Contents

Book Two: The Twelve Traditions

INTRODUCTION

Welcome! The book you have in your hands is a discussion of the Twelve Steps and Twelve Traditions of Narcotics Anonymous. We realize that, whether written or verbal, no discussion of something as personal and individual as recovery can be all things to all people. This book is not meant to be an exhaustive study of NA's steps and traditions, nor is it meant to be the final word on any aspect of recovery or NA unity. Rather, it is meant to help you determine your own interpretation of the principles contained in our steps and traditions. We hope you will find personal growth, understanding, and empathy in the following pages. We pray you will be moved to a new level of insight into your recovery and the valuable place you occupy as a member of Narcotics Anonymous.

Each member of NA has contributed to this book in some way. Whether you are new to recovery or one of our longtime members, your experience, your support, and, above all, your presence in the rooms where addicts meet to share recovery have been the motivating forces behind the production of this book. Though the process of writing a book about the experience of a fellowship as diverse as ours has been lengthy, we saw all the barriers and stumbling blocks fade away in the light of our primary purpose: to carry the message to the still-suffering addict. That one purpose, clear and powerful, stands alone in our collective consciousness as the only thing that really matters. With that, all is possible and miracles happen.

The nature of the recovery process gave us the title for this book. After all was said and done, one fundamental truth emerged as the crux of our program: IT WORKS. The reasons our program works, the how and why of recovery, are found in many places: in each other, in our relationship with a Higher Power, in our hearts and minds, and finally, in the collective wisdom of our members. Because our principal endeavor in the development of this book has been to capture that collective wisdom in written form, we believe the title of this book is most appropriate: It Works: How & Why.

We pray that this book truly represents the therapeutic value of one addict helping another. We offer this book as a gift, addict to addict, and hope our love and concern for every addict who is trying our way of life comes across as strongly as we feel it. Please use and enjoy this book. Share it with your friends, your sponsor, and the people you sponsor. After all, it is through sharing with each other that we find our own answers, our own Higher Power, and our own path of recovery.

BOOK ONE
The Twelve Steps

◇

The purpose of this portion of the book is to invite members to engage in a journey of recovery and to serve as a resource in gaining a personal understanding of the spiritual principles in the Twelve Steps of Narcotics Anonymous. This portion of the book explores the spiritual principles in each step and how we experience them in our lives. We believe that the steps are presented in a manner that encompasses the diversity of our fellowship and is reflective of the spiritual awakening described in our Twelfth Step.

STEP ONE

"We admitted that we were powerless over our addiction, that our lives had become unmanageable."

As addicts, we have each experienced the pain, loneliness, and despair of addiction. Before coming to NA, most of us tried everything we could think of to control our use of drugs. We tried switching drugs, thinking that we only had a problem with one particular drug. We tried limiting our drug use to certain times or places. We may even have vowed to stop using altogether at a certain point. We may have told ourselves we would never do the things we watched other addicts do, then found ourselves doing those very things. Nothing we tried had any lasting effect. Our active addiction continued to progress, overpowering even our best intentions. Alone, terrified of what the future held for us, we found the Fellowship of Narcotics Anonymous.

As members of Narcotics Anonymous, our experience is that addiction is a progressive disease. The progression may be rapid or slow, but it is always downhill. As long as we are using drugs, our lives will steadily get worse. It would be impossible to precisely describe addiction in a way that is agreeable to everyone. However, the disease seems to affect us in the following general ways. Mentally, we become obsessed with thoughts of using. Physically, we develop a compulsion to continue using, regardless of the consequences. Spiritually, we become totally self-centered in the course of our addiction. Looking at addiction as a disease makes sense to a lot of addicts because, in our experience, addiction is progressive, incurable, and can be fatal unless arrested.

In Narcotics Anonymous, we deal with every aspect of our addiction, not just its most obvious symptom: our uncontrollable drug use. The aspects of our disease are numerous. By practicing this program, we each discover the ways in which our addiction affects us personally. Regardless of the individual effects of addiction on our lives, all of us share some common characteristics. Through working the First Step we will address the obsession, the compulsion, the denial, and what many have termed a "spiritual void."

As we examine and acknowledge all these aspects of our disease, we start to understand our powerlessness. Many of us have had problems with the idea that, as addicts, we are obsessive and compulsive. The idea that these words applied to us may have made us cringe. However, obsession and compulsion are aspects of our powerlessness. We need to understand and acknowledge their presence in our lives if our admission of powerlessness is to be complete. Obsession, for us, is the never-ending stream of thoughts relating to using drugs, running out of drugs, getting more drugs, and so on. We simply can't get these thoughts out of our minds. In our experience, compulsion is the irrational impulse to continue using drugs, no matter what happens as a result. We just can't stop. We address obsession and compulsion here as they relate to our drug use because, when we first come into the program, our drug addiction is how we identify with each other and the program. As we continue in our recovery, we will see how these aspects of our addiction can manifest themselves in many areas of our lives.

Denial is the part of our disease that makes it difficult, if not impossible, for us to acknowledge reality. In our addiction, denial protected us from seeing the reality of what our lives had become. We often told ourselves that, given the right set of circumstances, we might still be able to bring our lives under control. Always skillful at defending our actions, we refused to accept responsibility for the damage done by our addiction. We believed that if we tried long and hard enough, substituted one drug for another, switched friends, or changed our living arrangements or occupations, our lives would improve. These rationalizations repeatedly failed us, yet we continued to cling to them. We denied that we had a problem with drugs, regardless of all evidence to the contrary. We lied to ourselves, believing that we could use again successfully. We justified our actions, despite the wreckage around us resulting from our addiction.

The spiritual part of our disease, the part we may recognize only by a feeling of emptiness or loneliness when we first get clean, is perhaps one of the most difficult aspects of addiction for us. Because this part of our disease affects us so profoundly and so personally, we may be overwhelmed when we think about applying a program of recovery to it. However, we need to keep in mind that recovery doesn't happen overnight for anyone.

As we start to look at the effects of our disease, we are sure to see that our lives have become unmanageable. We see it in all the things that are wrong with our lives. Again, our experiences are individual and vary widely from addict to addict. Some of us realized our lives had become unmanageable because we felt out of control emotionally or began to feel guilty about our drug use. Some of us have lost everything—our homes, our families, our jobs, and our self-respect. Some of us never learned how to function as human beings at all. Some of us have spent time in jails and institutions. And some of us have come very close to death. Whatever our individual circumstances, our lives have been governed by obsessive, compulsive, self-seeking behavior, and the end result has been unmanageability.

Perhaps we arrived in NA without recognizing the problems we had for what they were. Because of our self-centeredness, we were often the last ones to realize that we were addicts. Many of us were persuaded by friends or family to begin attending NA meetings. Other members received even stronger encouragement from the courts. No matter how it occurred, our long-standing illusions had to be shattered. Honesty had to replace denial before we could face the truth of our addiction. Many of us recall the moment of clarity when we came face to face with our disease. All the lies, all the pretenses, all the rationalizations we had used to justify where we stood as a result of our drug use stopped working. Who and what we were became more clear. We could no longer avoid the truth.

We have found that we cannot recover without the ability to be honest. Many of us came to NA after spending years practicing dishonesty. However, we *can* learn to be honest, and we must begin to try. Learning to be honest is an ongoing process; we are able to become progressively more honest as we work the steps and continue to stay clean. In the First Step, we begin to practice the spiritual principle of honesty by admitting the truth about our drug use. Then we go on to admit the truth about our lives. We face what *is*, not the way things could be or should be. It doesn't matter where we come from or how good or bad we think we've had it; when we finally turn to Narcotics Anonymous and the Twelve Steps, we begin to find relief.

As we begin working the First Step, it is important to ask ourselves some basic personal questions: Can I control my use of drugs? Am I willing to stop using? Am I willing to do whatever it takes to recover? Given a choice between finding a new way of life in NA and continuing in our addiction, recovery begins to appeal to us.

We begin to let go of our reservations, those parts of ourselves we won't surrender to the program. Most of us *do* have some reservations when we first get clean. Even so, we need to find ways of addressing them. Reservations can be anything: a belief that, because we never had a problem with one particular drug, we can still use it; placing a condition on our recovery, such as only staying clean as long as our expectations are met; a belief that we can still be involved with the people associated with our addiction; a belief that we can use again after a certain amount of time clean; a conscious or unconscious decision to work only certain steps. With the help of other recovering addicts, we can find ways to put our reservations behind us. The most important thing for us to know about reservations is that, by keeping them, we are reserving a place in our program for relapse.

Recovery begins when we start to apply the spiritual principles contained in the Twelve Steps of NA to all areas of our lives. We realize, however, that we cannot begin this process unless we stop using drugs. Total abstinence from all drugs is the only way we can begin to overcome our addiction. While abstinence is the beginning, our only hope for recovery is a profound emotional and spiritual change.

Our experience shows that it is necessary for us to be willing to do anything it takes to obtain this precious gift of recovery. In recovery, we will be introduced to spiritual principles such as the surrender, honesty, and acceptance required for the First Step. If we faithfully practice these principles, they will transform our perceptions and the way we live our lives.

When we first begin to practice these principles, they may seem very unnatural to us. It may take a deliberate effort on our part to make the honest admission called for in Step One. Even though we are admitting our addiction, we may still wonder if this program will really work. Acceptance of our addiction is something that goes beyond our conscious admission. When we accept our addiction, we gain the hope of recovery. We begin to believe on a deep level that we, too, can recover. We begin to let go of our doubts and truly come to terms with our disease. We become open to change. We surrender.

As we work the First Step, we find that surrender is not what we thought it was. In the past, we probably thought of surrender as something that only weak and cowardly people did. We saw only two choices: either keep fighting to control our using or just cave in completely and let our lives fall to pieces. We felt we were in a battle to control our using and that, if we surrendered, the drugs would win. In recovery, we find that surrender involves letting go of our reservations about recovery and being willing to try a different approach to living life. The process of surrender is extremely personal for each one of us. Only we, as individuals, know when we've done it. We stress the importance of surrender, for it is the very process that enables us to recover. When we surrender, we know in our hearts that we've had enough. We're tired of fighting. A relief comes over us as we finally realize that the struggle is over.

No matter how hard we fought, we finally reached the point of surrender where we realized that we couldn't stop using drugs on our own. We were able to admit our powerlessness over our addiction. We gave up completely. Even though we didn't know exactly what would happen, we gathered up our courage and admitted our powerlessness. We gave up the illusion that we could control our using, thereby opening the door to recovery.

Many of us begin the process of surrender when we identify ourselves at an NA meeting with our name and the words, "I am an addict." Once we admit that we are addicts and that we cannot stop using on our own, we are able to stay clean on a daily basis with the help of other recovering addicts in Narcotics Anonymous. The paradox of this admission is evident once we work the First Step. As long as we think we can control our drug use, we are almost forced to continue. The minute we admit we're powerless, we never have to use again. This reprieve from having to use is the most profound gift we can receive, for it saves our lives.

Through our collective experience, we have found that we can accomplish together what we cannot do alone. It is necessary for us to seek help from other recovering addicts. As we attend meetings regularly, we can find great comfort in the experiences of those traveling this path with us. Coming to NA has been described by many members as "coming home." We find ourselves welcomed and accepted by other recovering addicts. We finally find a place where we belong.

Though we are sure to be helped by the sharing we hear at meetings, we need to find a sponsor to help us in our recovery. Beginning with the First Step, a sponsor can share with us his or her own experience with the steps. Listening to our sponsor's experience and applying it to our own lives is how we take advantage of one of the most beautiful and practical aspects of recovery: the therapeutic value of one addict helping another. We hear in our meetings that "I can't, but we can." Actively working with a sponsor will give us some first-hand experience with this. Through our developing relationship with our sponsor, we learn about the principle of trust. By following the suggestions of our sponsor instead of only our own ideas, we learn the principles of open-mindedness and willingness. Our sponsor will help us work the steps of recovery.

Talking honestly with our sponsor about our drug use and how it affected our lives will help us work the First Step thoroughly. We need always remember where we came from and where our addiction took us. We have only a daily reprieve from our active addiction. Each day, we accept the fact that we cannot use drugs successfully.

The process of recovery isn't easy. It takes great courage and perseverance to continue in recovery day after day. Part of the recovery process is to move forward in spite of whatever may stand in our way. Because long-lasting change in recovery happens slowly, we will turn to the First Step again and again.

Even long periods of abstinence do not guarantee us continued freedom from the pain and trouble that addiction can bring. The symptoms of our disease can always return. We may find that we are powerless in ways we never imagined. This is where we begin to understand how the things we tried so hard to control are, in reality, completely beyond our control. No matter how our disease displays itself, we must take its deadly nature into account. As we do, we develop a fuller awareness of the nature of our disease.

The disease of addiction can manifest itself in a variety of mental obsessions and compulsive actions that have nothing to do with drugs. We sometimes find ourselves obsessed and behaving compulsively over things we may never have had problems with until we stopped using drugs. We may once again try to fill the awful emptiness we sometimes feel with something outside ourselves. Any time we find ourselves using something to change the way we feel, we need to apply the principles of the First Step.

We are never immune from having our lives become unmanageable, even after years of recovery. If problems pile up and our resources for coping with them dwindle, we may feel out of control and in too much pain to do anything constructive for ourselves. We feel overwhelmed by life, and that feeling seems to make everything worse. When our lives seem to be falling apart, we reapply ourselves to the basics of the NA program. We stay in close contact with our sponsor, work the steps, and go to meetings. We surrender again, knowing that victory lies in the admission of defeat.

The feeling of love and acceptance we find in the Fellowship of Narcotics Anonymous allows us to begin recovering from our addiction. We learn a new way to live. The emptiness from which we suffered is filled through working and living the Twelve Steps. We learn that our addiction is being addressed in all its complexity by this simple program. We have found a solution to our hopelessness.

There is a deeply spiritual nature to our program of recovery. The Twelve Steps of Narcotics Anonymous will take us on a journey that will far exceed our expectations. Working and living the steps will lead us to a spiritual awakening. Step One is the beginning of this spiritual journey. To get started on this journey, we must become willing to surrender to this program and its principles, for our future hinges on our willingness to grow spiritually.

We are starting a new way of life, one that offers great joy and happiness. However, recovery doesn't exempt us from pain. Living life on life's terms combines moments of happiness with moments of sadness. Wonderful events are mixed with painful ones. We will experience a full range of feelings about the events in our lives.

By honestly looking at what we have become in our addiction, we recognize the powerlessness and unmanageability of our lives. Moving beyond our reservations, we accept our addiction, surrender, and experience the hope that recovery offers. We realize that we can no longer go on as we have been. We are ready for a change. We are willing to try another way. With our willingness, we move on to Step Two.

STEP TWO

"We came to believe that a Power greater than ourselves could restore us to sanity."

Our surrender in the First Step leaves us with a deep need to believe that we can recover. This surrender makes it possible for us to feel hope. By admitting our own powerlessness, we open our minds to an entirely new idea: the possibility that something greater than ourselves might be powerful enough to relieve our obsession to use drugs. It is quite likely that, before coming to NA, we never believed in any power but our own willpower, and that had failed us. NA introduces us to a new understanding. We draw hope from this understanding and begin to comprehend what it means to believe that a Power greater than ourselves can restore us to sanity. We find additional hope by listening to other recovering addicts. We can relate to where they've been and draw hope from who they've become. We listen closely at meetings and become willing to apply what we hear to our own lives. As we begin to believe that there is hope for us, we also begin to trust the process of recovery.

Our White Booklet states, "There is one thing more than anything else that will defeat us in our recovery; this is an attitude of indifference or intolerance toward spiritual principles. Three of these that are indispensable are honesty, open-mindedness, and willingness." This doesn't mean we must be unfailingly honest, open-minded, and willing. We just have to try as best we can to practice these principles. As we first approach Step Two, we can practice the principle of honesty by acknowledging and sharing what we do or don't believe about a Power greater than ourselves. Developing our open-mindedness requires some effort, but we can practice this principle by listening to other recovering addicts share how they came to believe. For many of us, the willingness to try something new came about simply because we were so tired of our old ways. It seemed to us that, because our own power wasn't sufficient to restore our sanity, perhaps something else could, if we let it.

Many of us felt that insanity was too harsh a word to describe our condition. However, if we take a realistic look at our active addiction, we'll see that we have been anything but sane. For the most part, our perceptions were not based in reality. We viewed the world around us as a hostile environment. Some of us withdrew physically and had little, if any, contact with anyone. Some of us went through the motions of life but allowed nothing to touch us emotionally. Either way, we ended up feeling isolated. Despite evidence to the contrary, we felt that we were in control. We ignored or didn't believe the truths that were staring us in the face. We continued to do the same things and expected the results to be different. Worst of all was the fact that we continued to use drugs, regardless of the negative consequences we experienced. Despite the warning signs that our drug use was out of control, we continued trying to justify it. All too often, the result was that we could no longer face ourselves. When we take a realistic look at our lives, there can be no doubt that we desperately need a restoration to sanity.

Regardless of our individual interpretation of the term "restoration," most of us agree that, for us, it means changing to a point where addiction and its accompanying insanity are not controlling our lives. Being restored to sanity is a life-long process. Individually, we experience it differently at varying stages of our recovery, but we all can see some results of this process right from the beginning of our recovery. Initially, being restored to sanity means that we no longer have to use drugs. We go to meetings rather than isolating. We call our sponsor rather than sitting alone with painful feelings. We ask for our sponsor's guidance in working the steps, a real demonstration of sanity. We begin to believe that a powerful force can restore us to sanity. At long last, we feel hope for ourselves.

"We came to believe" implies a process. For some, this process is simple, and it may bring immediate results. Many of us arrived in NA so completely defeated that we were willing to try anything. Seeking help from a Power greater than ourselves may have been the best idea we had ever heard. However, the process of coming to believe can be difficult, even painful. Many of us have found that acting as if we believe is helpful. This does not mean we should be dishonest. Rather, it means that if we have doubts, we practice the program as if we believe we can be restored to sanity.

Belief in a Power greater than ourselves does not come easily to all of us. However, we have found an open mind indispensable when we approach this step. If we look around us, we find many reasons to believe. Our belief may simply be that we can recover from a life of active addiction. The freedom from the obsession to use may be our first experience of a Power greater than ourselves at work in our lives. Perhaps for the first time in many years, our obsession with drugs no longer controls our every waking moment. Knowing that we don't have to use today is a powerful belief in and of itself.

We start to develop faith through the process of coming to believe. It starts with hope. For some of us, this may be only a faint spark at first, perhaps just the thought that maybe, if we work this program, our lives will get better. Our hope turns to faith as our lives begin to improve. For many of us, faith can be described as a belief in something intangible. After all, who can logically explain the sudden lifting of an obsession to use drugs, yet this has happened for many of us. With our hope for a different life and the beginnings of our faith that recovery is possible, we start the process of coming to believe in a Power greater than ourselves.

We come from various walks of life and experience, so it is natural that we bring with us differing concepts of spirituality. In NA, no one is forced to believe any set ideas. Each one of us can believe in anything in which we want to believe. This is a spiritual program, not a religion. Individually, we cultivate our own beliefs about a Power greater than we are. No matter what we understand this Power to be, help is available to us all.

In the beginning, many of us turn to the group or the love we encounter in Narcotics Anonymous as our Higher Power. An NA group is a powerful example of a Power greater than ourselves at work. Often in desperation, we enter a room full of addicts who share their experience, strength, and hope with us. As we listen, we know with certainty that they have felt the hopelessness and remorse from which we, too, have suffered. As we observe other addicts practicing a new way of life without the use of drugs, we may come to believe that we, too, can recover. Watching other addicts stay clean is compelling proof of the existence of a Power greater than ourselves. We notice the acceptance that recovering addicts show each other. We watch as addicts celebrate lengths of clean time that we think will be impossible for us to attain. Perhaps someone hugs us and tells us to "keep coming back." Members give us their phone numbers. We feel the power of the group, and this helps us start to heal.

Many of us use spiritual principles as a power greater than ourselves. We come to believe that, by practicing these principles in our lives, we can be restored to sanity. This makes sense to us because we have tried many times to think ourselves into a better way of life. We usually had good intentions, but our day-to-day existence rarely measured up to those intentions. Trying it the other way, practicing a better way of life by living according to spiritual principles, will eventually have an effect on our thinking.

It is not necessary that we define for ourselves the entire concept of a Power greater than ourselves. Those of us with many years of recovery find that our understanding of a Higher Power changes over time. Our belief grows, as does our faith. We come to believe in a Power which can help us far more than we originally thought.

As we search for understanding of a Higher Power, we can talk with our sponsor and other recovering addicts. We may ask them what their idea of a Higher Power is and how they have arrived at it. This may open our minds to possibilities we hadn't considered before.

While it is useful to question others about their spiritual beliefs, we must remember that our understanding of a Power greater than ourselves is up to each individual. Others can help us. We may even adopt the ideas of someone else for a while or just believe that they believe. Eventually, however, we need to come to believe for ourselves. The need for our own sense of spirituality is too vital to our recovery for us to neglect this highly personal process.

For us, part of the process of coming to believe is accepting the evidence we see. Our addiction caused us to deny the truths we saw. But now, in recovery, we can believe what we see. At first, we open our minds and try something new, somehow believing that what we try might work. After we take a few small steps toward belief and trust and see results, we become willing to take bigger steps. We find that we are no longer acting as if we believe. Our belief is now reinforced with our own personal experience, some of which is unexplainable. We sometimes encounter remarkable coincidences in our lives that have no rational explanation. We don't need to explain or analyze these occurrences. We can simply accept that they happen and be grateful for them.

The longer we stay clean, the more evident it becomes that our addiction goes much deeper than the drugs we used. Much of our problem seems to center in our search for something to make us feel whole. It is a tremendous struggle to stop relying on our own reasoning and ask for help, especially given the self-centered nature of our disease. However, we are becoming open-minded. In realizing that we don't have all the answers, we begin to find some humility. We may not grasp the full impact of what being humble means, but our open-mindedness assures us that we have found and have begun to demonstrate this valuable quality.

Our humility and open-mindedness make us teachable. We allow others to share what has worked for them. This takes humility, for we must let go of our fears about how we may appear to others. Some of the strongest suggestions we may receive from other addicts are to attend meetings, ask for help, pray, and work the steps. Our experience has shown us that belief in a Higher Power leads us toward recovery in Narcotics Anonymous. People tend to live what they believe, and our newfound belief calls on us to live the program. No matter what we choose for our personal Higher Power, we've come to believe that NA works. We live what we believe by continuing on our path of recovery and working the Twelve Steps to the best of our ability.

Even after years clean, when we have been working a program of recovery and seeking change, we may at times experience periods when life seems meaningless. We may experience a sense of alienation too painful to ignore. At such times, we may find ourselves moving away from sanity, not toward it. We may begin to question our commitment to recovery. We can become obsessed with self-destructive thoughts. We may feel an urge to fall back on what seems easier: the familiar ways of our addiction. During these times, we need to renew our commitment to recovery. We trust that we are undergoing a fundamental transformation, even though we may not yet understand its full implication for our lives. As painful as it seems, we must change. If we trust that there is growth despite the pain, we can walk through these difficult periods more readily.

During these times, relying on the Second Step provides us with hope and reminds us that we are not alone. If things don't feel right, we take time to think and seek suggestions from our sponsor. We trust that with help from other recovering addicts and a Power greater than ourselves, we can be restored to sanity in all areas of our lives. We draw upon what we have learned from going to meetings and following directions. We accept that life on life's terms may not always be to our liking or, more importantly, to our understanding. Sanity often means that we don't act on our first impulse. We begin to make choices that help us rather than harm us. What worked for us in the beginning remains applicable, no matter how many years we have been clean. Once again, we reapply ourselves to the basics of this program: going to meetings, reaching out for help, and working the steps. Although we may feel despair, there is hope; a Power greater than ourselves is always available to us.

Along with the hope we derive from working Step Two, we find that our way of thinking is undergoing a radical change. The whole world looks different. Where before we had no reason to hope, we now have every reason to expect a dramatic difference in our lives. By being open-minded, we've opened ourselves to new ideas. We've stepped away from the problem and toward a spiritual solution.

This solution is evidenced by our open-mindedness and our willingness to believe in a Power greater than ourselves. We must now go on to Step Three to develop a relationship with the God of our understanding.

STEP THREE

*ide a decision to turn our will and our lives
    ɔ the care of God* as we understood Him."

The surrender we experience in Step One, coupled with the hope and belief we find in Step Two, make us ready and willing to continue on the path toward freedom in Narcotics Anonymous. In Step Three, we put our belief in a Higher Power into action, making a decision to turn our will and our lives over to the care of the God of our understanding.

Essential to working the Third Step is our willingness to allow the God of our understanding to work in our lives. We develop this willingness over time. The willingness we experience in our early recovery is valuable even though we may be willing only to a certain degree. Although this may feel like un-conditional willingness, many of us have discovered that our willingness grew as we learned to trust a Power greater than ourselves.

The decision we make in Step Three requires that we move away from our self-will. Self-will is composed of such characteristics as closed-mindedness, unwillingness, self-centeredness, and outright defiance. Our self-centered obsession and its accompanying insanity have made our lives unmanageable. Acting on our self-will has kept us trapped in a continuous cycle of fear and pain. We wore ourselves out in fruitless attempts to control everyone and everything.

We couldn't just allow events to happen. We were always on the lookout for ways we could force things to go as we wanted.

When we first look at making the decision called for in this step, we are likely to have questions, uncertainty, and even fear about what we are being asked to do. We might wonder why we need to make a decision to turn our will and our lives over to the care of the God of our understanding. Or we may wonder what will happen to us if we place ourselves in God's care. We may fear that we won't be happy with what our lives will be like after working this step.

When we trust that there is growth in taking action despite our fear or uncertainty, we are able to work Step Three. Even though we do not know how our lives will change as we work this step, we can learn to trust that our Higher Power will care for us better than we could. The Third Step is our commitment to our own emotional, physical, and spiritual well-being.

What began in the Second Step as belief in a Higher Power can become a fuller relationship with a God of our understanding in Step Three. The decision that we make by working this step, and the relationship that results, will revolutionize our existence.

This decision is easier to make than to live by. We can easily lapse into old behavior; it takes determination, time, and courage to change. Because we're not perfect, we simply continue to reaffirm our decision on a regular basis and then do the very best we can to live by it. Complete and unconditional surrender of our will and our lives is an ideal we strive to fulfill. Although we don't become perfect, we do make a profound change by working this step. We are making a serious effort to live differently than we have in the past. From now on, we are going to be practicing this decision, and the way we relate to the world around us can change radically as a result.

In working Step Three, we begin to learn how to stop struggling. We learn to let go and trust the God of our understanding. If we take time to think and seek direction before acting, we no longer have to run on our own self-centered will. Turning our will and our lives over to the care of our Higher Power provides a solution to the problems created by a life based in self-will, resentment, and control.

The spiritual principles we are practicing will guide us, not just in the Third Step but throughout our recovery. The first three steps provide us with the solid spiritual foundation we will need to work the rest of the steps. We keep our initial surrender alive by actively practicing the faith and willingness required to work the Third Step. In other words, we've admitted our powerlessness and inability to manage our own lives; we've come to believe; now we need to surrender to the care of the God of our understanding.

We may find the willingness to work the Third Step by remembering where we came from and believing that where we are going is certain to be quite different. Though we don't know what this "difference" will entail, we know that it is sure to be better than what we've had in the past. We rely on our faith and believe that this decision is one of the best decisions we've ever made.

Turning our will and our lives over to the care of the God of our understanding is a tremendous decision. We may very well wonder exactly how we are supposed to put this decision into practice. Because our individual beliefs about a Power greater than ourselves vary, there is no uniform way to put our decision into action. However, we have found some ways we all can use to find a personal understanding of the Third Step. One is to continue our efforts to develop a personal relationship with a God of our understanding. Another is to give up our efforts at controlling everything around us. We relax our grip on the burdens we've been carrying and turn them over to the care of a Higher Power. Yet another way we can practice our Third Step decision is to continue with our recovery by working the remainder of the steps. Our sponsor will guide us in applying the spiritual principles of recovery, showing us how to shift our focus away from our own self-interest and toward a more spiritually centered life.

As we get ready to make this decision, we talk with our sponsor, go to step meetings, and take the opportunity to share about it with other NA members. We gather as much knowledge, insight, and experience as we can from these sources, and then we make our own decision. No one can do it for us; we must consciously decide to do this for ourselves.

Of course, this is not a decision we make solely with our intellect. In truth, this is a choice we make with our hearts, a decision based much more in feeling and desire than in deliberate reasoning. Though the path from mind to heart seems a difficult one, formally working this step with our sponsor seems to help us make this decision a part of who we are.

The search for a God of our own understanding is one of the most important efforts we will undertake in our recovery. We have complete personal choice and freedom in how we understand our Higher Power. We can each find a Higher Power that does for us what we cannot do for ourselves. Because we are powerless over our addiction, we need a Power greater than ourselves to help us.

Just as our freedom to have a God of our own understanding is unlimited, so is our freedom to communicate with our Higher Power in whatever ways work for us. Anytime we communicate with our Higher Power, whether it's simply with our thoughts or aloud at the close of a meeting, we are praying. Most of us ask our Higher Power for direction on a daily basis.

Our relationship with our Higher Power grows stronger as we practice faith. In our experience, talking to a Power greater than ourselves works. When we are having trouble in a particular area of our lives or when we feel unable to stay clean, our Higher Power can help; we only need to ask. With our prayers, we ask a Power greater than ourselves to care for us. Each time we take this action, we strengthen our faith and our decision to rely on our Higher Power.

Step Three doesn't free us from having to take action, but it does liberate us from excessive worry about the results. If we want something—a job, an education, recovery—we have to make the effort to get it. Our Higher Power will take care of our spiritual needs, but we need to participate in our own lives; we can't simply sit back and expect God to do everything. We are responsible for our recovery.

Our lives are meant to be lived. No matter how sincere our efforts at "turning it over," we will make mistakes, wander off course, and experience moments of doubt. However, with each setback we are given a new opportunity to renew our commitment to live by spiritual principles. Part of the process of surrendering to God's will is to surrender to spiritual principles such as honesty, open-mindedness, willingness, trust, and faith. We try to align our actions with what we believe our Higher Power would want for us, and then we deal with life as it happens.

We may hesitate to work Step Three in all areas of our lives, especially in matters we want to control. Our experience has been that we tend to hold on to certain areas. Perhaps we think, "I can control my finances just fine" or "My relationship is working; why do I need to turn that over to the care of my Higher Power?" Working Step Three only in certain areas of our lives short-circuits our spiritual development. We have found that our recovery benefits when we practice the principle of surrender, to the best of our ability, in *all* areas of our lives. We strive to work this step thoroughly. We begin to see positive results from the decision we have made. We begin to notice changes. While the circumstances of our lives may not change, the way we deal with those circumstances does. Because we have made the decision to allow spiritual principles to work in our lives, we may notice a sense of relief. We are being relieved of a burden we've carried far too long: the need to control everything and everyone. We begin to react differently to the situations and people around us. As we gain acceptance, we cease to struggle against life on life's terms. Striving to maintain and build on our surrender, we are better able to live and enjoy life in the moment.

For some of us, deciding to turn our will and lives over to the care of the God of our understanding is a process, not an event. However, in making that decision, we do make a commitment to practice this step in our lives. When we are tempted to manipulate a situation, we recall this decision and let go. When we catch ourselves attempting to exert control over someone or something, we stop and instead ask a loving God to help us work this step.

Relinquishing control is not easy, but we can do it with help. With guidance from our sponsor and daily practice, we are sure to find ourselves learning how to get our egos out of the way so our Higher Power can work in our lives. Each time we are fearful over a situation, we can turn to this step and find the means to walk through our fear without resorting to our old ways.

Recovery doesn't exempt us from having to live through painful situations. At some point in our lives, we may have to mourn the death of a loved one or deal with the end of a relationship. When such things happen to us, we hurt, and no amount of spiritual awareness will take our pain away. We do find, however, that the caring presence of a loving Power greater than ourselves will help us get through our pain clean. We may find that we are able to feel our Higher Power's presence in the group, in our friends, or in talking to our sponsor. By tapping into that Power, we begin to trust and rely on it. We can cease questioning why painful things happen and trust that walking through the difficult times in our lives can strengthen our recovery. We can grow in spite of our pain or, perhaps, in response to it.

Recovery is a process of discovery. We learn about ourselves, and we learn how to cope with the world around us. When we are sincere in our desire to allow our Higher Power to care for us, we begin to gain a sense of serenity. We notice a gradual change in our thinking. Our attitudes and ideas become more positive. Our world is no longer as distorted by self-pity, denial, and resentment. We are beginning to replace those old attitudes with honesty, faith, and responsibility; as a result, we begin to see our world in a better light. Our lives are guided by our emerging integrity. Even though we make mistakes, we become more willing to take responsibility for our actions. We learn that we don't have to be perfect to live a spiritual life. When we work Step Three with an open mind and heart, we find the results are far beyond our expectations.

As we experience this new way of life, we begin to realize that recovery is a priceless gift. We learn to trust; as we do, we open the doors to intimacy and develop new relationships. Where once we focused only on not using, we now can appreciate the many things that make our lives so valuable. We savor the laughter and the joy we hear expressed so abundantly in our meetings. As recovery becomes more central in our lives and we internalize the principles embodied in the steps, our view of the world changes profoundly. As our awareness grows, so does our appreciation and faith in our Higher Power.

If we pause to reflect on our lives at this stage of our recovery, we will see that we have experienced dramatic personal growth. The relief we experience as a result of working the first three steps is only a glimpse of the growth we can experience through working the Twelve Steps.

The role of the Third Step expands in our lives as we continue working the other steps. Step Eleven asks us to pray for the knowledge of God's will for us and the power to carry it out. Step Three begins this process; it is here that we start to seek God's will for us. Moving from a self-seeking life to a life based on spiritual principles requires us to change profoundly.

With the help of a loving God, we are ready to move forward on our journey. This is a twelve-step program, not a three-step program. The decision we've made in the Third Step is perhaps the most momentous decision we'll ever make in our lives, but we need to work the rest of the steps for it to remain meaningful. There is more work to do. We have found that the spiritual path set forth in the Twelve Steps is the only way to recovery in Narcotics Anonymous. Putting our recovery commitment into action, we work Step Four.

STEP FOUR

*"We made a searching and fearless moral
inventory of ourselves."*

By working the first three steps, we have formed a
solid foundation for our recovery. Our active addiction
cannot remain arrested, however, unless we build
upon this foundation. As we worked the Third Step,
many of us were puzzled: How can we make sure we
are really turning our will and lives over to the care
of God? The answer is simple: We work the remainder
of the steps, starting with Step Four.

Why work the Fourth Step? After all, we've been able
to stay clean so far. But some of us are still haunted
by a driving obsession to use drugs. Others find that
the feelings of discomfort are more subtle: a nagging
feeling that something isn't quite right, a sense of
impending doom, or feelings of fear and anger that
have no apparent reason. Still others may think we're
doing just fine without a Fourth Step. However, our
experience as a fellowship has shown that, sooner or
later, members who don't work this crucial step
relapse.

For many of us, our motivation to work the Fourth
Step is quite simple: We're working a program of
recovery and we want to continue. Because our
disease involves much more than our drug use,
recovery involves more than simple abstinence from
drugs. The solution to our problem is a profound

change in our thinking and our behavior. We need to change how we perceive the world and alter our role in it. We need to change our attitude. Whether our motivation is a desire to move away from our addiction or to move toward recovery doesn't really matter.

The Fourth Step is a turning point in our journey of recovery. It is a time for deep personal reflection. The confusion that we attempted to mask with self-deception and drugs is about to diminish. We are embarking on a search for insight into ourselves, our feelings, our fears, our resentments, and the patterns of behavior that make up our lives.

We may be very frightened at the prospect of examining ourselves so thoroughly. We don't know ourselves very well, and we may not be sure we want to. Our fear of the unknown may seem overwhelming at this point, but if we recall our faith and trust in our Higher Power, our fear can be overcome. We believe that part of God's will for us is to work the steps. We trust that the final outcome of working the Fourth Step will be the continued healing of our spirits, and we go on.

The principles of recovery that we have already begun to practice are vital to working the Fourth Step. The honest acceptance of our addiction, brought with us from Step One, will help us to be honest about other aspects of our addiction. We've developed a level of trust and faith in a Power greater than ourselves, and that glimmer of hope we've been feeling is growing with each day clean. We've paved the way to recovery with our willingness, and we find the courage necessary to work the Fourth Step through living these principles. Honesty is an essential part of this step. Our years of living a lie must end. If we sit down and become very quiet with ourselves, we will find it easier to get in touch with the truth. What we currently know to be true, we put on paper, holding nothing back. Telling the truth is a brave act, but with our faith and trust in the God of our understanding, we find the courage we need to be searching and fearless. With our courage, we are able to put on paper those things we thought we'd never tell.

What is meant by a "searching and fearless moral inventory?" We take stock of our assets and liabilities. We try to get at the bottom of who we are, to expose the lies we have told ourselves about ourselves. For years, we became whoever we needed to be to survive our addiction. After living a lifetime of lies, we began to believe those lies. Although we did discover some valuable truths in the First Step, the Fourth Step further separates fantasy from reality. We can begin to stop being the person we have invented and find the freedom to be who we are.

If the word "moral" bothers us, we have found that talking with our sponsor about our reservations can ease our discomfort. A moral inventory doesn't mean that we will condemn ourselves. In reality, the inventory process is one of the most loving things we can do for ourselves. We simply look at our instincts, our desires, our motives, our tendencies, and the compulsive routines that kept us trapped in our addiction. No matter how many days or how many years we have been clean, we are still human and subject to defects and failings. An inventory allows us to look at our basic nature with its flaws and its strengths. We look not only at our imperfections, but also at our hopes, our dreams, our aspirations, and where they may have gone astray. Step Four is a big step forward on the path of recovery.

Some of us may want to write our inventory all at once; others spend some time writing each day. Any time we sit down to write, we ask our Higher Power for the courage and honesty we need to be thorough and to reveal what we are searching for. In most cases, we are relieved to find that once we begin, the words seem to flow naturally. We need not worry about what we are writing. Our Higher Power will reveal no more to us than we can handle.

Most of us don't have much experience with the type of self-appraisal we are about to do, and we must have the guidance and support of our sponsor in order to understand what we're doing. Our sponsor may give us a format to follow, certain subjects or points to concentrate on, or just general guidance. Not only can our sponsor provide direction for the actual inventory, he or she can encourage us to be courageous, remind us to pray, and be emotionally supportive throughout this process. We often strengthen our relationship with our sponsor by relying on her or his experience at this time. Consistent action on our Fourth Step is important. We can't afford to delay work on our inventory. Once we begin writing, we need to continue our inventory until we are done. If we have a tendency to procrastinate, it is a good idea to set aside a certain amount of time each day to work on our inventory. Such a routine establishes our inventory as a high priority in our lives. If we put our Fourth Step away once we have begun, we run the risk of never returning to it.

We are painstaking and detail-oriented in our inventory. We systematically examine all aspects of our lives. We begin to see and understand the truth about ourselves, our motives, and our patterns. It is important that we look at more than one dimension of our experience. What motivated us to act the way we did? What repercussions did our behavior have in our lives? How did our behavior affect those around us? How did we harm others? How did we feel about our actions and others' reactions? While these are only a few of the points we address in our inventories, we have found them and other issues like them to be essential areas to examine.

In the Fourth Step, it is important to take a good hard look at how fear has worked in our lives. Our experience tells us that self-centered fear is at the root of our disease. Many of us have pretended to be fearless when, in fact, we were terrified. Fear has driven us to act rashly in trying to protect ourselves. We have often been paralyzed into inaction because of our fears. We may have resorted to scheming and manipulating because we feared the future. We went to extremes to protect ourselves from what we saw as potential loss, disaster, and a constant lack of what we needed. In the past, we had no faith that a Higher Power would care for us; therefore, we attempted to take control of our lives and everything around us. We used people, we manipulated, we lied, we plotted, we planned, we stole, we cheated, and then we lied some more to cover up our schemes. We experienced envy, jealousy, and deep, gut-wrenching insecurities. We were alone. As we drove away the people who cared about us, we used more drugs, trying to cover up our feelings. The lonelier we felt, the more we tried to control everything and everybody. We suffered when things didn't go our way, but so strong was our desire for power and control that we couldn't see the futility of our efforts to manage events. In our new lives, we have faith in a loving God whose will for us is better than anything we could manipulate or control for ourselves. We need not fear what might happen.

In our inventories, we assess the emotional effects of our addiction. Some of us became so skilled at shutting down our feelings with drugs or other distractions that, by the time we came to our first meeting, we had lost touch with our own emotions. In recovery, we learn to identify what we are feeling. Naming our feelings is important, for once we do so, we can begin to deal with them. Rather than panicking over how we feel, we can specifically say how we're feeling. This gets us away from our limited way of identifying feelings as either "good" or "bad" with not much in between.

We make a list of our resentments, for they often play a large part in making our recovery uncomfortable. We cannot allow ourselves to be obsessed with hostility toward others. We look at the institutions that may have affected us: our families, schools, employers, organized religion, the law, or jails. We list the people, places, social values, institutions, and situations against which we bear anger. We examine not only the circumstances surrounding these resentments, but we look at the part we played in them. What in us was so threatened that we experienced such deep emotional torment? Often, we will see that the same areas of our lives were affected again and again.

We look at our relationships as well, especially the manner in which we related to our families. We don't do this to place blame for our addiction on our families. We keep in mind that we are writing an inventory of ourselves, not of others. We write about how we felt about our families and the way we acted on our feelings. In most cases, we'll find that the patterns of behavior we established early in life are what we've carried with us up to the present. Some of our patterns and choices have served us well, while others have not. Through the inventory, we search for the patterns we want to continue and those we want to change.

Writing about all of our relationships is very important, and we'll want to pay particular attention to our friendships. If we gloss over examining our platonic friendships in favor of focusing on romantic relationships, our inventories will be incomplete. Many of us come to NA never having had a long-term friendship because of conflicts within ourselves. Those conflicts were the real grounds for the arguments we started with our friends and our ensuing refusal to work through the disagreement and continue the friendship. Some of us felt that we would end up getting hurt in any close friendship, so before that happened, we arranged the end of the friendship ourselves. We may have feared intimacy to such a degree that we never revealed anything about ourselves to our friends. We may have induced guilt in our friends to ensure their loyalty or indulged in other forms of emotional blackmail. If our friends had others in their lives, we may have felt so jealous and insecure that we tried to remove the threat of their other friends. Our behavior ranged from taking our friends hostage to taking them for granted. We may find several instances where we sacrificed our friendships for romantic relationships.

We will probably find identical conflicts and behaviors in our romantic relationships. We'll see the same difficulties with trust, refusal to be vulnerable, and perhaps a lifelong pattern of inability to make commitments. As we write, we'll most likely see fear of intimacy in each relationship or discover that we've never understood the difference between intimacy and sex. Whether we ran from close relationships because of fear or because we had been hurt over and over again, we search out the common threads that appear in all of our relationships.

We may find that our sexual beliefs and behavior have caused problems in our relationships. We may have settled for sex when we really wanted love. We may have used sex to get something we wanted or believed that, by having sex, we could extract a commitment from an unwilling partner. We ask ourselves if our sexual behavior has been based in selfishness or in love. We may have used sex to fill the spiritual void we felt inside. Some of us felt shame as a result of our sexual practices. After years of compulsively acting on our fears and misguided beliefs about sex, we want to be at peace with our own sexuality. This is a very uncomfortable topic for most of us. However, if we want something different than what we've had, it's necessary that we begin the process of change by writing about it.

Some of us were abused. We may have been victims of incest or rape. We may have had terrible childhoods of deprivation and neglect. Experiences like these may have led us to inflict the same abuse on others. We may have prostituted ourselves or allowed other forms of degradation because we didn't feel that we deserved anything better. Though painful and sad, the past cannot be changed. However, the warped beliefs we have developed about ourselves and others *can* be changed with the help of our Higher Power. We write about events like these so that we can be free of our most painful secrets and get on with our lives. We don't have to be the lifelong victims of our past. To experience serenity, we must begin to alter the self-defeating patterns that have prevailed in our lives. The Fourth Step helps us identify those patterns. We begin to see how we have maneuvered through life, perhaps not consciously planning our own misery but making choices which resulted in our lives becoming unmanageable. Most of us have blamed various people for the prices we paid for our addiction. We didn't want to accept that our addiction had a negative impact that we alone were responsible for. Some of us committed crimes and then complained about the consequences. Some of us were irresponsible at work and then objected loudly when we were held accountable. We beat a hasty retreat whenever life caught up with us. Our inventories will help us identify our responsibility for our actions and find those circumstances where we tend to place blame elsewhere. Our booklet, *Working Step Four in Narcotics Anonymous*, can provide more avenues to explore.

The quality of our lives depends, to a large degree, on the results of our decisions. As we write our inventory, we look for the times when we made decisions that hurt us; we also look for those times when we made decisions that worked out well. If we lived our lives by default, refusing to make any choices, we write about that, too. Those times when we procrastinated until opportunities were missed and gone, the times when we abandoned all responsibility, the times when we withdrew and refused to participate in life—all are inventory material. Most of us had hopes and dreams for ourselves at some point in our lives, but we abandoned those in the pursuit of our addiction. In our inventory, we try to recall our lost dreams and find out how our choices had ruined our chances of having those dreams come true. We ask ourselves when we stopped believing in ourselves and when we stopped believing in anything outside ourselves. Through this process, our lost dreams may reawaken.

We dig deep to learn how we lived in conflict with our own morals and values. If we believed it was wrong to steal and we were stealing everything we could get our hands on anyway, what did we do to quiet our anguish? If we believed in monogamy but were unfaithful to our partners, what did we do so that we could live with our compromised principles? Certainly we used more drugs, but what else? We explore how we felt about ignoring our deepest beliefs. In the process, we discover our lost values so that we can begin to rebuild them.

In our inventories, we will need to be aware of our assets. With most of us being unaccustomed to looking for our character strengths, we might have some trouble with this task. But if we examine our behavior with an open mind, we're sure to find situations where we persevered in the face of adversity, showed concern for others, or even where our spirit triumphed over our addiction. We begin to uncover the pure and loving spirit that lies at the core of our being as we look for our character assets. We begin to define our values. We learn what we can do and, more importantly, what we can't do if we want to lead productive and fulfilling lives. What we did in our active addiction will not work for us in recovery. Step Four allows us to chart a new course for our lives.

The Fourth Step provides us with the initial insight we need to grow. Whether we are writing our first inventory or our twentieth, we are starting a process that takes us from confusion to clarity, from resentment to forgiveness, from spiritual confinement to spiritual freedom. We can turn to this process again and again. When we are confused, when we are angry, when we have problems that don't seem to disappear, an inventory is a good way to take stock of just where we stand on the path to recovery. After we have written a number of inventories, we may discover that our first Fourth Step merely scratched the surface. As different attitudes and behaviors become apparent to us in later recovery, we'll want to renew the process of change by working the Fourth Step again.

The steps are tools we use over and over on our spiritual path. In the process of our recovery, God will reveal more to us as we have the maturity and the spiritual strength to understand it. Over time, the nature of the work we have to do is disclosed to us. As we continue in recovery, we begin to resolve some of the basic conflicts contributing to our addiction. As the pain of old wounds begins to fade, we begin to live more fully in the present.

The Fourth Step allows us to identify the patterns, behaviors, and beliefs that show us the exact nature of our wrongs. We have written an inventory of ourselves which has revealed what we can change with God's help. To continue the process of change, we move on, making our admissions in Step Five.

STEP FIVE

*"We admitted to God, to ourselves, and to
another human being the exact nature
of our wrongs."*

Now that we have completed our written inventory,
it is essential that we share it promptly. The sooner
we work our Fifth Step, the stronger the foundation
of our recovery will be. We've built this foundation
on spiritual principles such as surrender, honesty, trust,
faith, willingness, and courage; with each step forward
in our recovery, we strengthen our commitment to
these principles. We reaffirm our commitment to
recovery by immediately working Step Five.

Despite our desire to recover, we may find that we're
feeling frightened at this point. This fear is only natural.
After all, we're about to confront the exact nature of
our wrongs, candidly admitting our secrets to God,
to ourselves, and to another human being. If we allow
our feelings of shame or our fears of change and
rejection to stop our progress, our problems will only
be compounded. If we stop moving forward in our
recovery, if we cease making every possible effort to
recover, we will have given in to the disease of
addiction.

We must overcome our fear and work the Fifth Step
if we are to make any significant changes in the way
we live. We gather our courage and go on. We may
call our sponsor for reassurance. Usually, a reminder

that we don't have to face our feelings alone makes all the difference in easing our fears. Working this step with the support of our sponsor and a loving God is a way of putting into practice our decision to allow God to care for our will and our lives. That decision, like most decisions we make, must be followed with action. Following our Third Step decision with the action of the Fourth and Fifth Steps will lead to a closer relationship with our Higher Power.

Our understanding of the spiritual principles we have practiced in the first four steps will be enhanced by working the Fifth Step. We experience honesty by making an admission, just as we did in Step One, but we experience it on a deeper level. The admission we are about to make to ourselves in Step Five is especially important. Not only do we open up and tell the truth about ourselves, we also hear this admission from our own lips, breaking the pattern of denial that has plagued us for so long. We find new levels of honesty, especially self-honesty, when we squarely face the results of our addiction and see the reality of our lives. The risks we take in this step increase our trust in God and nourish the faith and hope we first experienced in Step Two. We take our willingness a step further, thereby renewing the decision we made in Step Three. We draw on the courage we acquired in Step Four and find that we are far more brave than we ever dreamed possible. This bravery is demonstrated not by our lack of fear but by the action we take in spite of our fear. We set a time to share our inventory, then we show up and share at the scheduled time.

Another action which requires courage is our admission to ourselves. We need to focus particular attention on this aspect of the Fifth Step. If we don't, we may find the benefits we derive from this step are not as meaningful as they could have been. As our Basic Text states, "Step Five is not simply a reading of Step Four." We want to make sure we are acknowledging and accepting the exact nature of our wrongs. We can even formalize this admission to ourselves if we think it will help. However, the manner in which we make this admission to ourselves is not as important as the action itself.

We gain a new understanding of the principle of humility as we work this step. We've most likely been under the impression that we were somehow bigger or more visible than other people. Through working the Fifth Step, we find that few of our actions deserve exaggerated attention. Through our self-disclosure, we feel connected with humanity, perhaps for the first time in our lives.

As we share our most personal feelings and our most carefully guarded secrets, we may experience anguish. However, many of us have looked up and seen unconditional love in the eyes of the person hearing our Fifth Step. The feelings of acceptance and belonging we experienced at that moment helped us to feel a part of the program.

The knowledge that we are about to face feelings we have long avoided may cause a rise in our anxiety level, but we go on, encouraged by our sponsor to trust the God of our understanding. The first thing we must realize is that the Fifth Step is not a quick fix for a painful situation. If we work this step expecting our feelings to go away, we are expecting the steps to numb us the way drugs did. We review our first four steps and see that their purpose is to awaken our spirits, not deaden our feelings. We will need support and understanding to cope with our feelings. If we choose an understanding individual to make our admissions to, we will have all the support we need.

Although there is no requirement that the listener must be our sponsor, most of us choose to share our inventory with him or her. By doing so, we are most likely to benefit from the full range of experience another recovering addict has to share. After all, who can better understand what we are attempting than those who have done it for themselves? Addicts more experienced in recovery than we are will already have dealt with the matters we are just beginning to face. Such people can share with us their experience and the solutions they have found through working this step. The bond we share with our sponsor will strengthen our connection with the program and increase our sense of belonging.

The person who listens to our Fifth Step should be someone who understands the process of recovery we are involved in and someone who is willing to help us through it. We have found that an ideal listener will have enough compassion to honor our feelings, enough integrity to respect our confidences, and enough insight to help us keep the exact nature of our wrongs within our field of vision. Knowing that we are sharing *our* inventory, she or he will help us to avoid getting sidetracked by blaming others for the things we've written about in our Fourth Step.

Although we know we are going to derive meaningful benefits from working this step, we may still need to take a moment to reaffirm our surrender and the decision we made in the Third Step. We can ask a Power greater than ourselves for the honesty, courage, and willingness to work this step. To invite God into this process, we may want to say a prayer. The prayer can be anything that reaffirms our commitment to recovery. Praying with the person hearing our Fifth Step can be a profoundly intimate experience.

Not only do we pray to ask for strength and courage, many of us also ask our Higher Power to listen as we make our admission. Why is it so important that we also make our admission to God? Because this is a spiritual program, and our whole purpose is to awaken spiritually. Our willingness to approach our Higher Power openly with our past and who we are is central to our recovery. In the past, some of us felt that we weren't worthy of a relationship with God. Our secrets blocked our ability to feel any acceptance or love from that Power. When we reveal something about

ourselves, we draw closer to our Higher Power and
experience the unconditional love and acceptance
which springs from that Power. The feeling that the
God of our understanding accepts us, no matter what
we've done, enhances our acceptance of ourselves.
The positive relationship we are building with a Higher
Power carries over into our relationships with others
as well.

We may be surprised by the intensity of the
partnership we are developing with our sponsor as
we share our inventory. If we've never really been
listened to before, we may be startled to discover that
we are being asked questions about some fine point
of our personal history or that our sponsor is jotting
down notes while we share. Our self-esteem increases
as we realize that what we have to share is worth such
close attention. We may see deep compassion in our
listener's eyes, showing us that our pain is understood.
That compassion is one more assurance of the
presence of a Power greater than ourselves.

Looking at and sharing the *exact nature* of our wrongs
is not likely to be a comfortable activity. We have
looked back and seen how repeating the same
patterns over and over again has kept us stuck in the
same place. And we haven't just seen the surface
behavior; we've seen the defects of character that
have been behind our behavior all along. We start to
realize that there is a difference between our actions
and the exact nature of our wrongs. For instance, we
may see example after example of situations where

we lied in a vain attempt to make everyone like us. But those examples aren't the nature of our wrongs. The nature of these wrongs is the dishonesty and manipulation we were demonstrating each time we lied. If we look beyond the dishonesty and manipulation, we'll most likely find that we were afraid no one would like us if we told the truth.

As we share our inventory, our sponsor will sometimes share some of his or her own experience with us. Our sponsor may cry with us or smile in recognition at some of the struggles we are now sharing. We may laugh together as we share some of the more comical aspects of our addiction and the ridiculous lies we told ourselves so that we could continue to live as we were living. As we see how similar our feelings are to our sponsor's feelings, we realize that there are other people like us. We're human beings, nothing more, nothing less. Our self-obsession blinded us to this, making us feel unique. Suddenly we understand that other people, too, have painful problems and that ours are no more significant than anyone else's. Healing can take place when we see a glimpse of ourselves in the eyes of another. We find humility in that moment and a reason to hope that the serenity and peace we have been striving for are within our reach at last.

Our feelings of alienation fade as we experience an emotional connection with another human being. We are allowing someone entry to those places we've never before opened to another person. This may be the first time we've ever trusted another person enough to tell her or him about ourselves and allow that person to get to know us. We may be surprised at the closeness that develops between us and our sponsor. We're developing a give-and-take relationship based on equality and mutual respect, the kind that can last for a lifetime.

After working our Fifth Step, we may feel a little raw or emotionally vulnerable. We've taken a major step in the healing process of recovery. This process could be thought of as "surgery of the spirit." We've opened up old wounds. We've exposed our most carefully constructed lies for the deceptions they were, and we've told ourselves some painful truths. We've dropped our masks in the presence of another person.

At this point, we may experience a dangerous urge to run from our new awareness and return to the familiar misery of the past. We may feel tempted to avoid our sponsor because he or she knows all about us now. It is very important that we resist such impulses. We must talk with other recovering addicts about our fears and feelings so we can hear the experience they have to share. We'll find that what we're going through is not unique and feel relieved when others tell us they went through the very same struggles after they worked their Fifth Step.

Our awareness of our patterns of relating with others and the risk we have just taken in admitting them to another bring about a momentous breakthrough in our relationships. Not only do we form a close bond with our sponsor, but the risk we take in trusting this person will help us develop close relationships with others as well. We've risked trusting one person with our secrets and our feelings, and we haven't been rejected. We begin to have the freedom to trust others. Not only do we find out that others are trustworthy and deserve our friendship, we find that we are also trustworthy and deserving. We may have thought we were incapable of loving or being loved or ever having friends. We discover that these beliefs were unfounded. We learn, from the example of our sponsor, how to be a more caring friend.

Our relationships begin to change after this step, including the one we have with the God of our understanding. Throughout the process of the Fifth Step, we turned to that Power when we were fearful, and we received the courage we needed to complete the step. Our belief and our faith grew as a result. Because of this, we're willing to put more of ourselves into building a relationship with God. Just like any other relationship, the one we develop with our Higher Power calls for openness and trust on our part. When we share our most personal thoughts and feelings with our Higher Power, letting down our walls and admitting we are less than perfect, intimacy develops. We develop a certainty that our Higher Power is always with us and that we are being cared for.

The process we have undertaken so far has made us aware of the *exact nature* of our wrongs. The exact nature of those wrongs is our character defects. We now know that the patterns of our lives were rooted in dishonesty, fear, selfishness, and many other defects of character. We've seen the whole spectrum of our defects and are ready for something new. With this readiness, we move on to Step Six.

STEP SIX

*"We were entirely ready to have God remove
all these defects of character."*

The insight we gained in Step Five regarding the exact nature of our wrongs, while valuable, is only the beginning of the striking changes that take place in our lives as we move on to Step Six. The admission we made of the nature of our wrongs, our character defects, is necessary if we are to be ready to have them removed. Deeply shaken by our part in the past, we can expect our attitudes to be profoundly changed by working the Sixth Step.

Although some of us have not understood the critical importance of the Sixth and Seventh Steps, they are essential actions that must be taken if we expect to make any significant and lasting changes in our lives. We cannot simply say, "Yes, I'm ready. God, please remove my defects" and go on to Step Eight. If we gloss over the Sixth and Seventh Steps and go on to make our amends, we will only wind up owing more amends by repeating the same destructive patterns as before.

The lifelong process of the Sixth Step is just that—a process. We've started the process of becoming entirely ready, and we will strive to increase our readiness throughout our lifetime. Our job is to become entirely ready and to open our hearts and minds to the deep internal changes that can only be brought about by the presence of a loving God.

We've already had experience in the Third Step with what we must do now in the Sixth Step. Just as we surrendered our will and lives to the care of a Power greater than ourselves because we could no longer go on managing our own lives, we now prepare to surrender our defects of character to a loving God because we have exhausted our attempts to change on our own willpower. This process is difficult and often painful.

Our growing awareness of our defects often causes us pain. We've all heard the expression "ignorance is bliss," but we are no longer ignorant of our character defects, and this awareness hurts. All of a sudden, we'll notice a wounded look in the eyes of a friend after we've acted on one of our less endearing traits. We'll hang our heads in shame, mumble an apology, and probably beat ourselves inwardly for being so callous one more time. We feel sick inside, knowing how our actions adversely affect the people in our lives. We are sick and tired of being the people we have been, but this feeling compels us to change and grow. We want to be different than we have been in the past, and the good news is that we already are. Being able to see beyond our own interests and being concerned about the feelings of others are striking changes, considering that our raging self-obsession is at the core of our disease.

We are likely to feel very frustrated as we notice that our defects are getting in the way of our recovery. We may attempt to suppress them ourselves by either denying their existence or hiding them from others. We may think that if no one knows about them, our more unattractive characteristics will go away. What we must do, rather than try to exert power and control over our defects, is step out of the way and allow a loving God to work in our lives. One part of this process involves becoming responsible for our behavior.

When we are confronted with our character defects, either by our own insight or by someone we have hurt, we begin by taking complete responsibility for our actions. We don't avoid responsibility by saying something like, "Well, God hasn't removed that defect yet" or "I'm powerless over my defects, and that's just the way I'm going to be." We accept responsibility for our behavior—good, bad, or indifferent. We no longer have our drug use or our ignorance as an excuse to be irresponsible.

When we honestly admit our wrongs, we find humility. The humility we experienced in Step Five grows as we again sense our humanness and realize that we are never going to be perfect. We accept ourselves a little bit more, we surrender, and our willingness to change increases dramatically. We have already experienced remarkable changes in our emotional and spiritual nature through our continuous efforts to live by the principles contained in the previous steps. Despite our lack of familiarity with the realm of the spirit, we must remember that, in Steps One through Three, we were given the basic tools we need to negotiate the path of recovery. We carry within us the honesty it took to make our initial surrender, the faith and hope we developed in coming to believe in a Power greater than ourselves, and the trust and willingness required from us when we made our decision to turn our will and lives over to the care of God. Our hearts were touched by the humility of believing in that Power.

On this spiritual foundation we lay the principles of commitment and perseverance as we work the Sixth Step. We need the willingness to make a commitment to pursue our recovery despite the continued presence of character defects in our lives. We mustn't give up, even when we think no change has taken place. We are often blind to our own internal changes, but we can rest assured that what's happening inside us is evident on the outside to others. Our job is to keep on walking, even though it may feel as though each step requires more strength than we can muster. No matter how difficult our progress, we must persevere. We can make use of the sheer grit and tenacity it took to maintain our active addiction by being steadfast and strong in our efforts to sustain our recovery.

Having written our inventory and shared it with ourselves, the God of our understanding, and another human being, we've become aware of our defects of character. With the help of our sponsor, we write a list of those defects and focus on how they manifest themselves in our lives. Our character defects are basic human traits that have been distorted out of proportion by our self-centeredness, causing enormous pain to us and those around us.

Take a defect such as self-righteousness, for example, and imagine it in its normal, uninflated state—confident belief in one's own values. Strong, confident, and well-rounded people have formed values and principles to live by and believe deeply in their rightness. Such people live what they believe and share those beliefs with others in a non-critical way when asked. Confidence in our beliefs is essential. Without it, we would be wishy-washy, unsure of our decisions, and probably somewhat immature in our dealings with the world. Confident belief becomes ugly self-righteousness when we insist that others live by our values. Attempting to enforce our insistence by manipulating or exploiting others makes this defect even uglier.

Or consider fear. The absence of fear in the face of a personal attack, catastrophic illness, or potential injury would signal insanity rather than serenity! We all have fears—of being alone, of not having our physical needs met, of dying, and many others. But when our fears become obsessively self-centered, when we spend all of our time protecting ourselves from what *might* happen, we can no longer deal effectively with life in the here and now.

As we work Step Six, bridging the vast gulf that lies between fear and courage requires a great deal of willingness and trust on our part. Our fears of what we will be like without relying on the destructive behavior of our past must be overcome. We will need to trust our Higher Power to remove our defects of character. We must be willing to take a chance that what lies beyond the Sixth Step is going to be better than our current stock of fears, resentments, and spiritual anguish. When the pain of remaining the same becomes greater than our fear of change, we will surely let go.

We may wonder what will happen to us without the use of what we may see as survival skills. After all, in our active addiction, our self-centeredness protected us from feeling guilt and enabled us to continue our drug use without regard for those around us. Our denial protected us from seeing the wreckage of our lives. Our selfishness made it possible for us to do whatever it took to continue in our insanity. But we no longer need these "skills." We have a set of principles to practice that are much more appropriate to our new way of life.

As we write our list of defects and see how they have been at the root of our troubles, we need to be open-minded about how our lives would be without these defects. If one of our character defects is dishonesty, we can think about situations in our lives where we normally lie and imagine how it would feel to tell the truth for a change. If we put some effort into this exercise, we may feel a sense of relief at the possibility of a life free from having to cover small deceits with major fabrications and all the complications inherent in dishonesty. Or, if we find defects based in laziness and procrastination, we can visualize leaving behind our marginal existence and moving on to a life of realized ambitions, new horizons, and unlimited possibilities. In addition to our hopes and dreams for the future, we might find in our sponsor or others whose recovery we admire more concrete examples of those assets for which we are striving. If we know members who are exhibiting the spiritual assets we want to attain, we can use them as an example for ourselves. What we hope to become is evidenced all around us in recovering addicts living by spiritual principles. Our sponsor and other members share the freedom they have found from their defects of character, and we have faith that what happened for them will also happen for us.

Even so, we may still go through a period of mourning over the loss of our illusions and old ways. Sometimes giving up those outdated survival skills feels like giving up our best friend. We do, however, need to surrender our reservations, excuses, rationalizations, and self-deceptions and go forward into recovery with our eyes wide open. We are completely aware that there's no turning back, because we can never forget the miracle that's begun to happen to us. Our bruised and battered spirits have started to heal in the course of working the steps.

Part of the process of becoming entirely ready involves practicing constructive behavior. Because we now understand and recognize our destructive behaviors, we'll find the willingness to practice constructive behaviors instead. For instance, if we're hurt somehow, we don't have to curl up in a ball of self-pity, complaining about what a rotten deal we got. Instead, we can accept what is and work toward finding solutions. The more we do this, the more we form a habit of thinking constructively. It becomes natural to begin examining alternatives, setting goals, and following through in the face of adversity. We don't have to spend time sulking or pointlessly complaining about circumstances beyond our control. We may even surprise ourselves with our cheer and optimism at times, and it's no wonder, considering how foreign such attitudes have been to most of us!

There may still be times when we feel that entirely too much is being asked of us. Many of us have exclaimed, "You mean I even have to tell the truth about *that*?" or "If only I could still lie, steal, or cheat, it would be so much easier to get what I want." We're torn between the unprincipled ways of our addiction and the character-building principles of recovery. While, at first glance, it may seem easier to manipulate outcomes or avoid consequences, we know that we cannot afford the price we would have to pay. The resulting shame, regret, and loss of spiritual contentment would far outweigh anything we might possibly gain by compromising our principles.

Through upholding the principles of recovery, we seek a life of harmony and peace. The energy we once put into the care and feeding of our character defects can now be put into nurturing our spiritual goals. The more attention we focus on our spiritual nature, the more it will unfold in our lives.

We will not, however, achieve a state of spiritual perfection, regardless of how diligently we apply the Sixth Step to our lives. We will most likely see the defects we deal with today manifest themselves in a variety of ways throughout our lifetime. Even after years of recovery, we may feel devastated at the reappearance of some old defect we thought had been removed. We are humbled by our imperfection—but let there be no mistake; humility is the ideal state for an addict to be in. Humility brings us back down to earth and plants our feet firmly on the spiritual path we are walking. We smile at our delusions of perfection and keep on walking. We're on the right path, headed in the right direction, and each step we take brings progress.

We gain more tolerance for the defects of those around us as we work this step. When we see someone acting out on a defect that we have acted on ourselves, we feel compassionate rather than judgmental, for we know just exactly how much pain such behavior causes. Rather than condemning the behavior of another, we look at ourselves. Having experience in accepting ourselves, we can extend compassion and tolerance to others.

We ask ourselves if we are entirely ready to have God remove all of our defects—every single one. If any reservation exists, if we feel the need to cling to any defect, we pray for willingness. We open our spirits to the healing we've found in Narcotics Anonymous and use the resources of our recovery to do our best each moment. Although the process lasts a lifetime, we only live in the present day. We've taken a giant step forward in the process of recovery, but it must be followed with another to be truly lasting. With the readiness we have at hand today, we go on to Step Seven.

STEP SEVEN

"We humbly asked Him to remove our shortcomings."

In Step Four, we uncovered the basic defects of our character. In Step Five, we admitted their existence. In Step Six, we became entirely ready to have them removed so that we could experience continued spiritual growth and recovery. Now, in Step Seven, we humbly ask our Higher Power to remove our shortcomings. When we ask our Higher Power to remove these shortcomings, we ask for freedom from anything which limits our recovery. We ask for help because we cannot do it alone.

Through working the previous steps, we see that attaining humility is necessary if we are going to live a clean life and walk a spiritual path. An attitude of humility is not the same as humiliation, nor is it a denial of our good qualities. On the contrary, an attitude of humility means that we have a realistic view of ourselves and our place in the world. In the Seventh Step, humility means understanding our role in our own recovery, appreciating our strengths and limitations, and having faith in a Power greater than ourselves. To work the Seventh Step, we must get out of the way so that God can do God's work. Humbly asking for the removal of our shortcomings means we are giving complete license to that loving Power to work in our lives, believing that God's wisdom far exceeds our own.

Even though we now possess some measure of humility, many of us may be somewhat confused by the word "humbly." We may have taken it for granted that God would remove our shortcomings immediately upon request. Those of us with this attitude may have been surprised when our Higher Power didn't comply with our request. On the other hand, some of us tried pleading with God to remove our shortcomings, guessing that would be a demonstration of humility.

We tried so hard to get it right. We were tired of our shortcomings. We were worn out from trying to manage and control them, and we wanted some relief. Oddly enough, this is precisely the attitude we hope to demonstrate in Step Seven, the attitude of humility. We admit defeat, recognize our limitations, and ask for help from the God of our understanding.

Asking our Higher Power to remove our short-comings requires a surrender of a more pronounced nature than our initial surrender. That surrender, born of sheer despair over our powerlessness and inability to manage our lives, moves into an entirely new realm in the Seventh Step. In this new level of surrender, we accept not only our addiction but also the shortcomings related to our addiction. Accepting our addiction was the first move in the direction of accepting ourselves. We know something about ourselves because of our work in the previous steps, and our illusions of uniqueness have been overcome in the process. We know that we are neither more nor less important than anyone else. Understanding that we are not unique is a good indication of humility.

Patience is an essential ingredient of working this step. We may have difficulty with the notion of patience because our addiction accustomed us to instant gratification. But we've already been practicing the principles that make it possible for us to be patient. We simply need to expand on our Third Step decision to trust the God of our understanding with our will and our lives. If we only trusted that Power to a certain extent in Step Three, it's time to increase our trust.

Because our view of what we can hope for may be limited, many of us can't even begin to imagine what our Higher Power has in store for us. If this is the case for us, we must rely on faith. As in the previous steps, we simply have to believe that God's will for us is good. Our faith gives us reason to hope for the best.

In working this step, we move away from intellectualizing the recovery process. Our concern is not to determine exactly how or when our shortcomings will be removed. It's not our job to analyze this step. This step is a spiritual choice, a choice that goes beyond any emotional reaction or conscious act of will. To choose to bypass it would leave us with only a heightened awareness of our character defects and no hope for relief from those shortcomings. The resulting pain might well be unbearable.

We've seen our character defects, our faulty belief systems, and our unhealthy patterns of behavior.

We've seen that we need to change but may not be aware that we've been changing since we first came to Narcotics Anonymous for help. We walked into our first meeting with a spiritual void. Some essential ray of spiritual light had been cut off. We had lost the ability to love, to laugh, and to feel. For so long, people had looked into our eyes and had trouble seeing the human being behind the blank gaze. From our very first meeting, we sensed the love and acceptance of other NA members. We began to come back to life. What we are experiencing is an awakening of the spirit—no less dramatic than it sounds. This awakening has been evident to those around us for quite some time, but the change is now so obvious that we can see it as well.

One of the changes we see is in our relationship with the God of our understanding. Previously, we may have felt that God was far removed and did not have much to do with us on a personal level. We may have had trouble grasping the fact that each one of us could have a God of our understanding always available to us. Prayer may have felt artificial for quite a while, but we may now sense that we are being listened to and loved when we pray.

Developing a relationship with the God of our understanding goes a long way toward increasing our level of comfort when we ask to have our shortcomings removed. The work we've done in the previous steps has enriched that relationship. We've asked our Higher Power for honesty, open-mindedness, and willingness, and we have been provided with the ability to develop those attributes that are so vital to our recovery.

Each time we come up short on any of the qualities we are trying to attain or when we have difficulty practicing spiritual principles, we turn to the God of our understanding. In this step, we ask a loving God to remove our impatience, our intolerance, our dishonesty, or whatever shortcoming is currently in the way. We find that our Higher Power always provides us with what we need, and our faith grows as a result. When we ask our Higher Power to remove our shortcomings, we may see little bits of some of them removed. Other defects may simply be shoved out of the way for a time so that we can move forward on the path of recovery. We may even attain complete freedom from having to act on those defects. The point is that we have come to believe that only the God of our understanding has the power to remove our shortcomings. We can actually ask our Higher Power to remove our shortcomings in good faith, knowing that it will happen in God's time. This faith can transcend our own ideas of what we need or think we should have.

Regardless of how secure we feel in our relationship with the God of our understanding, we need our sponsor to guide us through the Seventh Step. Our sponsor helps us with our understanding of humility and in finding a comfortable way of communicating with our Higher Power.

We need to remember that we are praying to a Power greater than ourselves. We ask humbly, knowing that we are powerless. Some of us will recite a formal prayer that demonstrates humility when we ask our Higher Power to help us. Some of us will pray in a more casual manner, just as humbly, but using our own words. Any communication with our Higher Power is prayer. However we choose to communicate with the God of our understanding, we feel a certain comfort come over us as we pray. We know that we are being cared for.

With this knowledge comes freedom. Though not a cure by any means, working the Seventh Step gives us the freedom to choose. We know that if we live by the spiritual principles of recovery, we no longer need to wear ourselves out trying to arrange situations and outcomes. We trust the God of our understanding with our lives. We may still be fearful from time to time, but we no longer have to react to fear in destructive ways. We have the freedom to choose to act constructively or, when appropriate, do nothing at all. Believing that we are being cared for is a result of developing a relationship with a Power greater than ourselves. We are in the process of developing a conscious contact with a Higher Power. We will strive to improve that contact throughout our lives. We are conscious of the God of our understanding and feel that Power's presence.

The process of the Seventh Step brings about a peace of mind that we never dreamed possible. We sense that what is present throughout our search for spiritual growth is our ability to feel our Higher Power's love for us. We glimpse a vision of complete freedom from our shortcomings. It doesn't matter that we will not attain a state of perfection or complete humility in our lifetime. The ability to contemplate this grand vision and meditate upon it are rare and priceless gifts in their own right.

We are being changed. We've not only heard about the miracle of recovery; we are becoming living, breathing examples of what the power of the NA program can do. The spiritual life has ceased to be a theory we hear about in meetings; it is now becoming a tangible reality. We can see a miracle simply by looking in the mirror. The God of our understanding has taken us from spiritually unconscious, hopeless addicts to spiritually aware, recovering addicts eager to live. Although we've reached this point, the damage caused by our shortcomings needs to be addressed. Desiring continued recovery and freedom, we go on to Step Eight and begin to make amends for the damage we've caused.

STEP EIGHT

"We made a list of all persons we had harmed and
became willing to make amends
to them all."

In the previous steps, we began to make peace with our Higher Power and with ourselves. In the Eighth Step, we begin the process of making peace with others.

By acting on our character defects, we inflicted harm on ourselves and those around us. In the Seventh Step, we asked our Higher Power to remove our short-comings. However, in order to gain true freedom from our defects, we need to accept responsibility for them. We need to do whatever we can to repair the harm we've done. In Step Eight, we begin to rectify our wrongs. We begin to accept responsibility for our actions by listing all the people we have harmed and by becoming willing to make amends to them all.

While our efforts to make amends may make a difference in the lives of those we have harmed, this process has its greatest impact on our own lives. Our objective is to begin clearing away the damage we've done so that we can continue with our spiritual awakening. By the time we work our way through the process of making amends, we will surely be astounded by the level of freedom we feel.

We are involved in a process designed to free us from our past so that we are able to live fully in the present. Many of us are haunted by memories of our mistreatment of others. Those memories can creep up on us without warning. Our shame and remorse over our past actions are so deep that these recollections can cause us to feel unbearable guilt. We want to be free of such guilt. We begin by making a list of the people we've harmed.

Just thinking about our list may frighten us. We may be afraid that we've done so much damage that we can never repair it, or we may be afraid of facing the people we've harmed. We find ourselves wondering how our amends will be received. Our most hopeful projections probably entail being absolved of any wrongdoing. Our most nightmarish expectations may involve someone refusing to accept our amends, preferring instead to take revenge. Most of us have fairly vivid imaginations, but this is not the time to get ahead of ourselves. We must avoid projections, either negative or positive, about actually making our amends. We are on the Eighth Step, not the Ninth Step. At this point, making a list and becoming willing to make amends are our only concerns.

Working the previous steps has prepared us for the willingness we need to begin the Eighth Step. We've honestly assessed the exact nature of our wrongs and examined how our actions affected others. It was not easy to admit our wrongs. We had to believe in a Power that would supply us with courage and love us through the pain involved in reviewing the results of our addiction. The same honesty and courage we called upon as we wrote our inventory and shared it are just as vital in making our amends list. We've been practicing these principles all along and are quite familiar with them. The Eighth Step is simply a continuation of our efforts to find freedom by applying spiritual principles.

Making the list and becoming willing may be difficult unless we overcome our resentments. Most of us owe amends to at least one person who has also harmed us. Perhaps we haven't truly forgiven that person yet and find we are very reluctant to put her or his name on our list. However, we must. We are responsible for our actions. We make amends because we owe them. We must let go of resentments and focus on our part in the conflicts in our lives. We won't get better and be able to live the spiritual life we are seeking if we are still in the grip of self-obsession. We let go of our expectations, and we let go of blaming anyone for our actions. Our idea that we have been a victim must go. In the Eighth Step, we are not concerned with what others have done to us. We are concerned only with accepting responsibility for what we've done to others.

If we still bear anger toward some of the people in our past, we will need to practice the spiritual principle of forgiveness. Our ability to forgive comes from our ability to accept and be compassionate with ourselves. However, if we have difficulty, we can ask our Higher Power for help. We pray for whatever it takes to become willing to forgive. We've begun to accept ourselves as we are. Now we begin to accept others as they are.

In developing a list of all the people, places, and institutions to whom we owe amends, we may wish to review our Fourth Step. If we've done a thorough Fourth Step, it should clearly outline our part in the conflicts in our lives and show how we harmed others by acting on our defects of character. We find the people we wounded with our dishonesty, the people we stole from or cheated, the people who were on the receiving end of our wrongs. We also take note of how we harmed society as a whole and add that to our list. We may have drained community resources, exhibited offensive behavior in public, or refused to contribute to the general welfare.

Although we may find the majority of our amends list from reviewing our Fourth Step, Step Eight isn't simply a restatement of our inventory. We are now looking for the people, places, and institutions we harmed, not just the types of harm we inflicted. We didn't just lie; we lied to *someone*. We didn't just steal; we stole from various *people*.

The writing we did on our Fourth Step is not the only source of help we will be given in compiling our amends list. Our sponsor can also help us. When we shared our inventory, our sponsor helped us focus on the exact nature of our wrongs. Our sponsor's insight helped us see how we had wounded people by acting on our character defects; that same insight will now help us determine who actually belongs on our amends list.

Many of us had trouble seeing how we had harmed ourselves and may have been surprised when other addicts suggested that we add our own name to the list. Many of us have gone to extremes in matters of accepting responsibility for ourselves. Some of us have had a tendency to deny any responsibility, while others have taken on total blame for every disagreement. As we talk with our sponsor and other addicts, our flawed perceptions begin to fall away and we find the clarity we need to work the Eighth Step. With the help we have received, we start to develop a realistic view of where our responsibility truly began and ended.

Before we proceed in making a list, it is important that we understand what the word "harm" means in the context of the Eighth Step. We may be inclined to think of harm only in terms of physical suffering. However, there are many different forms of harm: causing mental anguish, property damage or loss, inflicting long-lasting emotional scars, betraying trust, and so forth. Though we may exclaim, "But I never meant to hurt anyone!", this is beside the point. We are responsible for the harm we caused no matter what our intentions were. Any time when people were hurt in any way because of something we did, they were harmed. To gain a better understanding of how we may have harmed people, we may want to "put ourselves in their shoes." If we can imagine what it felt like to be the victim of our reckless disregard for those around us, we shouldn't have any trouble adding those names to our list.

In addition to understanding what harm means, we also need to understand what "make amends" means. This step does not say that we become willing to say we're sorry, although that may be a part of our amends. Most of the people we've hurt have probably heard us say "I'm sorry" enough to last a lifetime. In truth, we are becoming willing to do anything possible to repair the damage we've done, particularly by changing our behavior.

There may be instances in which we inflicted harm so severe that the situation simply can't be set right. This may be readily apparent as we look at our relationships with those who have been in our lives for quite some time. Over the years, we have involved our families, partners, and long-term friends in one painful situation after another. Even though we can't undo the past, our experience has shown that we still need to look at what we've done and acknowledge the damage we've caused. Despite the impossibility of changing what happened, we can start to make amends by not repeating the same behavior.

Accepting the harm we caused, being truly sorry, and becoming willing to go to any lengths to change is a painful process. But we need not fear our growing pains, for our acknowledgment of these truths helps us continue our spiritual awakening. Simply accepting the harm we caused increases our humility. Being truly sorry is a clear indication that our self-centeredness has diminished. Willing to go to any lengths to change, we are newly inspired.

Some of our willingness will come about simply by writing our amends list. We will have the opportunity to face the harm we've done. Some of us, after writing the name of a person to whom we owe amends and what we did to harm that person, have added plans for how we intend to make amends. Planning how we are going to make amends may help increase our willingness as we see that we do have the potential to repair the harm we've caused.

We want to become willing to make the amends we owe, and we do whatever it takes to gain that willingness. If we find ourselves engaging in debates with ourselves or getting caught up in assessing the exact level of willingness we need, we can lay these counter-productive thoughts aside by making a conscious decision to pray for willingness. We may still be slightly hesitant, but we do the best we can. Our recovery is at stake. If we want to continue with our recovery, we must make amends.

We ask God to help us find the willingness to make our amends. Praying for willingness takes our relationship with the God of our understanding a step further. In the Seventh Step, we furthered our personal relationship with our Higher Power by asking for freedom from our shortcomings. Now we trust that Power to provide us with whatever we need to work the Eighth Step. Our commitment to recovery includes becoming ready to go as far as we must.

A Higher Power is working in our lives, preparing us to be of service to others. The changes brought about by that Power are evidenced by our changing attitudes and actions. We are developing the ability to choose spiritual principles over character defects and recovery over addiction. We have a fresh outlook on life, and we know that we are responsible for what we do. We no longer feel constant regret over the harm we caused in the past. Simply understanding how badly we've hurt people, being truly sorry for the pain we've caused, and becoming willing to let them know of our desire to make things right are the keys to freedom from our past. Though we have yet to make peace with others, we've come a long way toward making peace with ourselves. With our new perspective, our trust in the God of our understanding, and our willingness, we go on to Step Nine.

STEP NINE

*"We made direct amends to such people
wherever possible, except when to do so
would injure them or others."*

Now that we are willing to make amends to all the
people we've harmed, we put our willingness into
action by working the Ninth Step. We're involved in
a process that takes us from awareness of our wrongs
and the conflicts they've caused, to a growing freedom
from those conflicts and toward the serenity we are
seeking. This process has called on us to examine our
lives, identify our character defects, and become
aware of how we harmed others when we acted on
those defects. Now we must do everything we can to
repair the harm we've caused.

We have our Eighth Step list, and we know what we
have to do; however, knowing and doing are two
different things. We may have a perfectly good plan
for making our amends but, when the moment arrives,
find ourselves overwhelmed by fear and feel unable
to go on. We may be afraid of how our amends will
be received. We may be worried that someone will
retaliate. On the other hand, we may be harboring a
secret hope that we will be excused from our
responsibilities. We cannot base our willingness on
the expectation that we won't actually have to make
restitution. For each of our amends, every possibility
exists, from being held fully accountable to being

completely excused. We must be willing to follow through, regardless of the potential outcome. Once again, with the help of our Higher Power, we simply have to walk through our fear and go on.

We must be courageous when we work this step. Though the prospect of making amends may frighten us, we turn to the God of our understanding for strength. Our Higher Power is with us as we make each of our amends. We rely on the presence of that Power, no matter how scared we are about approaching the people we have harmed.

We may hesitate, fearing other people won't accept us as readily as our fellow NA members have. However, we have found that recovering addicts don't hold a monopoly on kindness or forgiveness. Other people are capable of accepting us as we are and understanding our problems. But whether they are willing to accept us or not, we must go on with making our amends to them. The risk we take is sure to be rewarded with increased personal freedom.

The spiritual principles of honesty and humility that we've learned in earlier steps are invaluable to us in the Ninth Step. We would never be able to approach the people to whom we owe amends in the spirit of humility if we hadn't been practicing these principles before now. The honest examination we used to write our inventory and make our admissions, the ego-deflation brought about by our work in the Sixth and Seventh Steps, and the realistic look at how we harmed others have all worked together to increase our humility and provide us with the motivation needed to work the Ninth Step. Our path has led us to humbly accept who we have been and who we are becoming, resulting in a sincere desire to make amends to all those we have harmed. This desire to make amends should be the primary motive for working the Ninth Step. Making amends isn't something we do simply because our program of recovery suggests it. To be certain our motives are based in spiritual principles, we find it helpful to reaffirm our decision to turn our will over to the care of the God of our understanding before making each of our amends. A Power greater than ourselves will provide us with the guidance we need.

We should not expect a "pat on the back" or praise for living in accordance with the principles of recovery. People may respond to our amends in many different ways. They may or may not appreciate our amends. The relationships we have with those people may get better, or they may not. We may be thanked, or we may be told, "It's about time you did this." We must let go of any expectations we have on how our amends will turn out and leave the results to the God of our understanding. It is very important that we do our absolute best to make amends. Once we have done that, however, our part is finished. We can't expect our amends to magically heal the hurt feelings of someone we have harmed. We may humbly ask for forgiveness but, if we don't receive it, we let that expectation go, knowing we have done our best. As we are making amends, we ask ourselves if we are doing this because we are truly sorry and have a genuine desire to make reparations for what we've done. If we answer ''yes'' to this question, we can be assured that we are approaching our amends in the true spirit of humility and love.

Keeping our humility in focus, we ask for help from our sponsor. Whenever possible, we discuss each of our amends with our sponsor *before* we set out to make it. We tell our sponsor what we are making amends for, what we are planning to say, and what we intend to offer to set the situation right. What we intend to offer as amends should be appropriate to the harm we caused. For instance, if we borrowed money from someone and never paid it back, we don't merely apologize; we pay the money back. We talk directly to the person we harmed and amend exactly what we did wrong.

When we make amends to those we have held a resentment against in the past, an attitude of humility is imperative. We don't want to go to someone, intent on making amends, and end up in a shouting match over who was injured more severely. Even though we are sure to have amends to make to people who have also harmed us, we must set our hurt feelings aside. Our responsibility is to make amends for what *we* have done wrong, not to force others to admit how they have wronged us.

In our experience, making amends is a two-stage process. Not only do we make amends to the person we've harmed, we follow up on those amends with a serious change in our behavior. We mend our fences and we mend our ways. For example, some of us may have destroyed someone's property while we were angry. When we make our amends, we not only apologize to the person and replace or repair the property, we back that up by repairing our attitudes. We amend our behavior, making a daily effort not to express our anger by damaging property any more.

Changing the way we live is a lifetime process and is perhaps the most significant amends we can make. Some of the people we've harmed, like our families or others we've been close to for a long time, have suffered for years. Amends of this nature can't be made in a five-minute apology, no matter how heartfelt. Although an admission of wrong and an apology may be the starting point, we need to go on by making a concerted daily effort to stop hurting our loved ones. If we have neglected our families, we start spending time with them. If we have been thoughtless, always forgetting birthdays and anniversaries, we begin to be thoughtful instead, remembering those important events. If we have been inconsiderate, always wrapped up in what we wanted and needed, we now begin to be sensitive to the needs of others.

Of course, we may not have an ongoing relationship with some of the people we have harmed. For instance, if we are divorced from a spouse with whom we had children, we may owe child-support payments. Making such amends does not require that we rekindle an emotional relationship with our ex-partner. Remembering that our obligations are more than financial, we can work out a mutually acceptable plan to fulfill those obligations to our children.

Because the action we take in this step can have a profound impact on other people, we don't want to just carelessly step out and start making our amends without first discussing them in detail with our sponsor. Some of us have felt compelled to make our amends on an impulse, just to ease our own conscience; however, we usually ended up doing more harm than good. Suppose that, in our Fourth Step, we wrote about people we had secretly resented for years. Unbeknownst to those people, we had ridiculed, judged, and condemned them or otherwise defamed their character to others. Because all that character assassination was taking place behind those people's backs, do we now go to them and confess? Certainly not! The Ninth Step is not designed to clear our conscience at the expense of someone else. Our sponsor will help us find a way to make appropriate amends without causing additional harm.

Though it seems obvious that we wouldn't make direct amends in a situation where we would injure someone, we may find that we have questions about how to make "direct" amends when the person to whom we owe them is deceased, impossible to find, or lives thousands of miles away. There are many ways to make effective direct amends without doing it in person. If someone to whom we owe amends is deceased, we may find it very effective to write a letter saying everything we would say if the person were still alive. Then, perhaps, we may read that letter to our sponsor. It may be a noble desire to want to make amends in person to someone who lives thousands of miles away, but most of us lack the means to travel great distances solely for that purpose. In such situations, a telephone call or letter could serve the same purpose as an amends made in person. The people on our list who we can't find should remain on our list. An opportunity to make amends may present itself later on, even years later. In the meantime, we must remain willing to make those amends. Of course, we should never avoid making amends in person only because we are afraid of facing the person we have harmed. We make every effort to find the people we have harmed and make the best amends we can make.

Choosing the best way to make amends requires careful consideration and time spent searching our conscience for what is right. Some of us have to face situations that can't be corrected. Our actions may have left permanent physical or emotional scars or even caused someone's death. We must somehow learn to live with such things. We live with indescribable remorse over such acts and wonder what we could possibly do to make amends. This is where we have no choice but to rely on our Higher Power. We may have difficulty in forgiving ourselves, but we can ask for the forgiveness of a loving God.

We sit down, become quiet in the presence of our Higher Power, and ask for guidance in what we should do. Many of us have found answers in dedicating our lives to helping other addicts and other forms of service to humanity. There are no easy answers for problems like these; we simply do the very best we can, relying on our sponsor and the God of our understanding for guidance.

For many of us, the wreckage of our past includes such relatively minor things as outstanding arrest warrants for traffic violations, while others have committed crimes entailing very serious consequences. We may find ourselves in a dilemma over such issues. If we turn ourselves in to the authorities, we may go to jail. If we don't, we may live in fear of being caught and sent to jail anyway. With the help of our sponsor and the God of our understanding, we are willing to do whatever it takes to maintain our recovery. We may also have to rely on legal advice before making such amends. Consulting a lawyer about these problems can be of great benefit.

Especially troublesome financial amends may also require professional advice. Many of us have amassed debts at an alarming rate. We may owe financial amends that are beyond our means to pay in the foreseeable future. Some of us may owe bills that amount to more than we can conceivably earn in the next several years. Some of us rarely paid our rent, utility bills, or phone bills. We may have found it easier to uproot our lives and move rather than meet our financial obligations.

Just as we do for all of our amends, we discuss our financial amends with our sponsor first. Some of us have begun providing for our families since we've been in recovery; they are dependent on us for their food and shelter. We usually find that we have to budget our money very carefully in order to meet our current living expenses while paying as much as possible on our old debts. We may resolve such situations by contacting our creditors, explaining our situation, and expressing our desire to settle our debts. We agree on a reasonable plan for paying off our debts, and we stick to it. This is an example of how living our amends is a process rather than a "once and for all" occurrence. It takes great discipline, personal sacrifice, and commitment to continue to pay a bill for years and years, but we can regain our self-respect only by following through.

Most of us find making amends for the damage we did in intimate relationships to be extremely uncomfortable. As we wrote our Fourth Step, we realized that we not only robbed ourselves of the chance for meaningful relationships, we also caused deep emotional wounds in our partners. Our fears of intimacy or commitment may have led us to use, be unfaithful to, or abandon the people who loved us. We were generally unavailable to those people. While there are times when we need to approach such people with our amends, there are other times when it is best to leave them alone so as not to reopen old wounds. Knowing the difference requires complete honesty on our part and open communication with our sponsor. Whether or not we make direct amends to the people we've harmed in relationships, we definitely need to change the way we behave in our relationships today. If we ran from intimacy before, we need to sit down and learn to communicate with our partners. We must become more considerate, sensitive, and attentive to the needs of others.

Sometimes, the only way we can make amends is to change the way we live. As discussed in the Eighth Step, we may owe amends to our community or society as a whole. Though this may seem to be an abstract concept, we must make concrete amends by changing our behavior. If we harmed society, we start to make amends by becoming a productive member of society. We contribute. We look for ways to give, not take.

Our recovery is also a way of making amends to ourselves. We treated ourselves horribly in our active addiction. The guilt and shame we felt each time we harmed another human being took quite a toll on our self-respect. Our addiction humiliated us in a thousand different ways. Now, in recovery, we learn to treat ourselves in ways that demonstrate our self-respect.

The most important results of the Ninth Step will be found within ourselves. This step teaches us a great deal about humility, love, selflessness, and forgiveness. We begin to heal from our addiction and no longer live with as many regrets. We grow spiritually and find that we are truly gaining a new level of freedom in our lives. Our past is just that: the past. We have put it behind us so that it no longer hovers on the edge of our thoughts, waiting for a chance to haunt our present.

One of the most wonderful gifts we derive from working the Ninth Step is the knowledge that we are becoming better human beings. We realize how much we have changed because we are no longer doing the things for which we are making amends. We may not have realized how much we had changed in our recovery until now. The amends process drives home the knowledge that we are becoming truly different people. The extended nightmare of our addiction is finally beginning to fade in the dawning light of our recovery.

Our humility increases as we face the people we have harmed. The impact of realizing how deeply our actions have affected other people shocks us out of our self-obsession. We begin to understand that other people have real feelings and that we are capable of hurting them if we are careless. We learn about being considerate of other people as we work this step, and what we learn is what we practice in our lives today. It becomes natural for us to think before we speak or act, keeping in mind that what we say or do is going to affect our friends, our families, and our fellow NA members. We approach people with love and kindness, carrying within ourselves a deep and abiding respect for the feelings of others.

Because of the humility and selflessness so necessary in making our amends, we may be surprised at the way Step Nine enhances our self-esteem. One of the most paradoxical aspects of our recovery is that by thinking of ourselves less, we learn to love ourselves more. We may not have expected our spiritual journey to lead to a fresh appreciation of ourselves, but it does. Because of the love we extend to others, we realize our own value. We learn that what we contribute makes a difference, not just in NA but in the world at large.

As a result of working the Ninth Step, we are free to live in the present, able to enjoy each moment and experience gratitude for the gift of recovery. Memories of the past no longer hold us back, and new possibilities appear. We are free to go in directions we never considered before. We are free to dream and to pursue the fulfillment of our dreams. Our lives stretch out before us like a limitless horizon. We may stumble from time to time, but the Tenth Step gives us the opportunity to pick ourselves up and keep walking forward. Our Higher Power has given us an invitation to live, and we accept it with gratitude.

STEP TEN

"We continued to take personal inventory and when we were wrong promptly admitted it."

Recovery in Narcotics Anonymous is about learning how to live. Incorporating the spiritual principles we learned in the first nine steps into our lives has made it possible to live in harmony with ourselves and others. Self-examination, confronting what we find in ourselves, and owning up to our wrongs are critical elements of conducting our lives on a spiritual basis. By working the Tenth Step, we become more aware of our emotions, our mental state, and our spiritual condition. As we do, we find ourselves constantly rewarded with fresh insight.

Some of us look back at our Fourth Step and wonder why we have to do a Tenth Step. We may think that we've corrected all our past mistakes in the previous steps; since we have no intention of making those mistakes again, why should we continue with this relentless self-examination? The Tenth Step seems like a tiresome chore to some of us, a painful exercise that we could just as well avoid. But we must continue to grow, and that's exactly what the Tenth Step helps us do. Though we will return to the previous steps again and again, the Tenth Step furthers our spiritual healing in a different way: by creating an awareness of what's going on in our lives today.

The importance of keeping in touch with our thoughts, attitudes, feelings, and behavior cannot be overemphasized. Every day, life presents us with new challenges. Our recovery depends on our willingness to meet those challenges. Our experience tells us that some members relapse, even after long periods of clean time, because they have become complacent in recovery, allowing their resentments to build and refusing to acknowledge their wrongs. Little by little, those small hurts, half-truths, and ''justified'' grudges turn into deep disappointments, serious self-deceptions, and full-blown resentments. We can't allow these threats to compromise our recovery. We have to deal with situations such as these as soon as they arise.

In the Tenth Step, we use all the principles and actions we learned in the previous steps, applying them to our lives on a consistent basis. Beginning our days by reaffirming our decision to live life according to our Higher Power's will has helped many of us keep spiritual ideals foremost in our minds throughout the day. Even so, we are bound to make mistakes that are very familiar to us. We can attribute virtually every wrongdoing to a character defect we identified in the Sixth Step. Humbly asking the God of our understanding to remove our shortcomings is just as necessary now as it was in the Seventh Step.

In the Tenth Step, we take such actions on a regular basis. Each day, we take our own inventory, look for those times when we fall short of our spiritual ideals, and renew our efforts to live a principle-centered life. For example, when we are faced with the tendency to behave compulsively, ignoring the consequences of our actions, we need to focus on spiritual principles, take prompt action, and continue forward in our recovery.

Although forming a habit of working this step may be difficult at first, we must persist. We can set aside some time during the day for focused self-appraisal while gradually moving toward a goal of being able to look at ourselves throughout the day. We keep going forward, striving each moment to become ever more aware of ourselves. We need to develop self-discipline; the more effort we put into doing so, the more we'll find that working the Tenth Step will become as natural as breathing.

Not that we should be hard on ourselves, picking at our every motive and looking for problems where none exist. We need to stay in tune with the voice of our conscience and listen to what it's telling us. When we get a nagging feeling that something isn't quite right, we should pay attention to it. If our feelings of guilt or anger seem to go on for a long time, we can do something about them. We know when something is bothering us—perhaps not immediately, but usually not too long after the fact. As soon as we become aware that we're feeling ill at ease, we search out the cause and deal with it as soon as possible.

While we strive to maintain ongoing awareness throughout the day, it is also helpful to sit down at the end of each day and quietly reflect on what has happened and how we responded to it. Often, our sponsor will suggest that we write out our Tenth Step. We may also make use of our informational pamphlet, *Living the Program*. In this step, we ask ourselves the same types of questions we asked in the Fourth Step; the only difference is that the emphasis is on *today*. We look at our current behavior and ask ourselves if we are living by our values. Am I being honest today? Am I maintaining personal integrity in my relations with others? Am I growing, or am I slipping back into old patterns? We concentrate on the overall picture of our day.

In order to examine our day—or our life, for that matter—in its entirety, we have to draw on the humility we've acquired in the previous steps. We have learned quite a bit about ourselves: how we've responded to life in the past and how we want to respond to life now. It takes a great deal of awareness to humbly acknowledge our part in our own lives.

We may have trouble knowing when we are wrong simply because we usually intend to be right. For instance, at some point in our recovery, we may attend a group business meeting firmly convinced that we know what the group should do. We've studied all sides of the issues. We forcefully share our views at the meeting. We're so convinced of our rightness that we fail to recognize our self-righteousness. We are blind to the harm we're causing others by not respecting their views as much as our own.

Often we act in ways that are contrary to our values, yet we expect others to live up to our standards. For instance, we may find ourselves flinching when we hear others gossiping about someone. Following such an occurrence, we are likely to be self-righteous—until we catch ourselves doing the very same thing. Other situations can occur when we become supercritical of others. For example, we may have a tendency to have high expectations of others; however, we have a variety of excuses at hand for why these standards don't apply to us! If we find ourselves in the midst of such moral uncertainty, we can use the principles of the Tenth Step to provide more clarity.

There may be other times in our lives when we find ourselves in a situation that seems to require a compromise of our personal beliefs and values. For instance, if we had gained employment at a company only to discover that our employer expected us to indulge in questionable business practices, we could reasonably expect to feel confused about the choices available to us. Deciding what to do about such a difficult dilemma would be a tough decision for any one of us. We may be tempted to make a snap judgment or expect our sponsor to provide an easy answer; however, we have found that no one can solve such a dilemma for us. While our sponsor will provide us with guidance, we must apply the principles of the program for ourselves and arrive at our own decision. In the end, we are the ones who must live with our conscience. In order to do so comfortably, we must decide what is, and what is not, morally acceptable in our lives.

It can be very confusing to determine when we were wrong, especially when we're right in the middle of a conflict. When our emotions are running high, we may not be able to take an honest look at ourselves. We can see only our immediate wants and needs. At such times, our sponsor may suggest that we take a personal inventory on a particular area of our lives so that we can see our part. If our friends notice that we're acting on a character defect, they may suggest that we talk to our sponsor about it. Being open-minded to the suggestions of our sponsor and our NA friends, paying attention to what our conscience is telling us, spending some quiet time with the God of our understanding—all these things will lead us to greater clarity.

Once we're aware that we've been wrong—whether it's five minutes, five hours, or five days after the fact— we need to admit our error as soon as possible and correct any harm we've caused. As in the Ninth Step, we find that the process of admitting our mistakes and changing our behavior brings about tremendous freedom.

Of course, we must be just as careful when amending our current behavior as we were when we made amends in the Ninth Step. For instance, if we find that we were wrong because we sat in a meeting silently judging someone who shared, we certainly don't need to go tell that person what we were thinking. Instead, we can make an effort to be more tolerant.

We must remember that the Tenth Step isn't a one-sided endeavor, an exercise in noting what we have done wrong. We must resist any urge to become obsessive with this step, ruthlessly searching out every flaw in our character. The point of the Tenth Step is for us to be willing to pay attention to our thoughts, behaviors, and values, then work on what we need to change. We should acknowledge that, quite often, our motives are good and we do things right. Character defects and character assets do not exclude each other, and we are sure to find both on any given day.

We develop recovery-oriented goals for ourselves as we work this step. When we see that we've been afraid to go forward in a particular area of our lives, we can resolve to take a few risks, drawing our courage from our Higher Power. When we see that we've been selfish, we can strive to become more generous in the future. When we realize today that we've fallen short in any area of our lives, we don't have to be overwhelmed by feelings of dread and fear of failure. Instead, we can be grateful for our self-awareness and begin to feel a sense of hope. We know that, by applying our program of recovery to our short-comings, we will change and grow.

We begin to see ourselves more realistically as a result of working the Tenth Step. Many of us have remarked on the freedom we experienced through freely admitting our mistakes and releasing ourselves from unrealistic expectations. Where before we went from one extreme to another, either feeling better than everyone else or feeling worthless, we now find the middle ground where true self-worth can flourish. We feel renewed hope as we uncover long-neglected assets in this step. We see ourselves as we really are, accepting our good qualities along with our defects, knowing we can change with the help of a Higher Power. We are becoming what we were meant to be all along: whole human beings.

Although all of us need the love and attention of others, that doesn't mean we must depend on people to provide what we can only find within ourselves. We can stop making unreasonable demands on others and begin to give of ourselves in relationships. Our romantic relationships, our friendships, and our interactions with family members, co-workers, and casual acquaintances are undergoing an astounding change. We are free to enjoy another's companionship because we're no longer so obsessed with ourselves. We finally see that all the devices we use to keep other people away are unnecessary at best and, more often than not, are the underlying cause of the pain we suffer in our relationships.

Healthier relationships are just one indication that the quality of our lives has improved dramatically. Such indications merely reflect the intangible but very real changes that have taken place inside us. Our entire outlook has changed. Compared to the spiritual values we hold dear today, concerns such as "looking good" or amassing material wealth pale in significance. By accepting the challenge of self-appraisal called for in the Tenth Step, we've discovered that we value our recovery and our relationship with the God of our understanding above all else.

As the inner chaos that we lived with for so long subsides, we begin to experience long periods of serenity. During these times, we experience the powerful presence of a loving God in our lives. We are increasingly conscious of that Power and are ready to search for ways to maintain and improve our contact with it. Seeking direction and meaning for our lives, we go on to the Eleventh Step.

STEP ELEVEN

"We sought through prayer and meditation to
improve our conscious contact with
God as we understood Him, praying only
for knowledge of His will for us
and the power to carry that out."

Throughout our recovery, one of the things which stands out as a result of our working the steps is our success in building a relationship with the God of our understanding. Our initial efforts resulted in the decision we made in the Third Step. We continued by working the following steps, each one of which were designed to clear away whatever barriers might stand between our Higher Power and ourselves. As a result, we are open to receive our Higher Power's love and guidance directly into our lives.

For many of us, the characteristics of our disease and the things we did in our active addiction separated us from our Higher Power. Our self-obsession made it difficult for most of us to even believe in a Power greater than ourselves, much less achieve conscious contact with that Power. We could see no purpose or meaning in our lives. Nothing could begin to fill the emptiness we felt. It seemed as though we shared no common bond with others at all. We felt alone in a vast universe, believing nothing existed beyond what our limited view allowed us to see.

However, once we begin to recover, we find our obsession with ourselves diminishing and our awareness of the presence of a Higher Power growing. We've begun to see that we aren't alone and never have been. Through working the previous steps, we have already achieved a conscious contact with the God of our understanding. Our separation and isolation have ended. In the Eleventh Step, we now seek to *improve* our conscious contact with the God of our understanding through prayer and meditation.

Many of us had trouble understanding the meaning of "praying for power" in the Eleventh Step. At first glance, this seemed to contradict the most basic aspect of our recovery program: our admission of powerlessness. But if we take another look at the First Step, we'll see that it says we were powerless over our addiction, not that we won't be given the power to carry out the will of the God of our understanding. We did begin at a point of powerlessness in the First Step; we were powerless over our addiction and incapable of carrying out any will but our own. This doesn't mean we gain power over our addiction in the Eleventh Step. In the Eleventh Step, we pray for a particular kind of power: the power to carry out God's will.

We no longer shy away from spiritual growth because it has become so essential to maintaining the peace of mind we've found. Perhaps at the beginning of our recovery we worked the steps because we were in pain and afraid we would relapse if we didn't. But today we are motivated less by pain and fear, driven more by our longing for continued recovery.

This leaning toward recovery reveals that we've surrendered more completely. We've reached a state where we actually believe that the will of a Power greater than ourselves is better for us than our own will. It has become second nature for us to ask ourselves what our Higher Power would have us do in our lives rather than attempting to manipulate situations so they happen according to our ideas of what's best. We no longer see God's will for us as something we have to *endure*. On the contrary, we make a conscious effort to align our will with our Higher Power's, believing that we'll gain more happiness and peace of mind by doing so. This is what surrender is: a heartfelt belief in our own fallibility as human beings and an equally heartfelt decision to rely on a Power greater than our own. Surrender, the stumbling block of our addiction, has become the cornerstone of our recovery.

However, we cannot recover on surrender alone. We must build on our surrender by taking action, just as we have in the previous steps. In the Tenth Step, we began to practice the discipline required to live spiritually on a daily basis. We continue practicing this principle in the Eleventh Step by persisting in our efforts to take action each day. We place prayer and meditation high on our priority list. We resolve to make prayer and meditation as much a part of our daily routine as eating and sleeping, and then we employ the necessary self-discipline to achieve our resolve.

To work this step, we must also increase the courage we've developed in the previous steps. Though the courage we demonstrated when we honestly and thoroughly examined ourselves was beyond anything we had previously experienced, we now need to develop a markedly different form of courage. We need the courage to live according to spiritual principles, even when we are afraid of the results. Despite our fear, we do what's necessary and draw on the endless well of courage we can find by tapping into a Power greater than ourselves.

With all this discussion of God, we may again find ourselves growing uncomfortable, perhaps wondering if this is where the "religious catch" we've anticipated is going to be revealed. We may wonder if our sponsor is now going to inform us that we must pray or meditate in a particular way. Before we get carried away with such fears, we would do well to remember one of the basic principles of recovery in Narcotics Anonymous: our absolute and unconditional freedom to believe in any Higher Power we choose and, of course, our right to communicate with our Higher Power in whatever way conforms to our individual beliefs. Although some of us practice a traditional religion, only rarely do we hear specific religious beliefs discussed in our meetings. We respect the rights of our members to form their own spiritual beliefs and tend to frown on anything with the potential to dilute the spiritual message of recovery.

In this encouraging atmosphere, most of us find it relatively easy to discard our preconceived ideas of the "right" way to pray or meditate. Finding our own way is another matter. We may have a basic understanding of what prayer and meditation are, prayer being the times we talk to a Higher Power and meditation the times we listen for a Higher Power's answers. We may not be aware of the many options that are open to us. Searching those options out and exploring their usefulness to us can be uncomfortable and time-consuming. It is only by being open-minded and by taking action that we are likely to find what is right for us as individuals. We may experiment with a whole assortment of practices until we find something that doesn't feel foreign or contrived. If we have found that *everything* feels strange, then we practice a form of prayer and meditation until it no longer seems unnatural. Many of us have adopted an eclectic approach, borrowing our practices from a variety of sources and combining those which provide us the greatest comfort and enlightenment.

We are on a spiritual path which will lead us to a greater understanding of our Higher Power. Many of us have remarked on the great joy we find along the way. We are sure to get help from our fellow members or, perhaps, even from others who are also walking a spiritual path. Seeking out these individuals and asking for their guidance can help us find our own answers; however, sharing in another's experience does not excuse us from the need to seek our own. Others may be able to show us the path they walked, sharing with us the joy and insight they found along the way; nevertheless, we may find our spiritual paths taking a different turn and have to adjust our method of travel accordingly. In the end, we find what's true for us in moments of personal contact with our Higher Power. The experience shared by others is just that: *experience*, not ultimate answers to the mysteries of life.

Our understanding of a Higher Power grows and changes through prayer and meditation. We find that it is too limiting to define our Higher Power in such a way that our understanding is set in stone once and for all. An interesting parallel can be drawn if we remember the times we've thoughtlessly tossed other human beings into categories and left them there. We deprived ourselves of an opportunity to know someone else on a deeper level. Treating our Higher Power as something to be defined will rob us on a grand scale, halting further spiritual growth the minute we arrive at an absolute definition.

In addition to the open-mindedness so necessary to working the Eleventh Step, it is vital that we actively pursue knowledge of God's will for us and the power to carry it out. This knowledge is what we are searching for when we pray, whether our prayers are desperate pleas or calm requests for guidance. Regardless of our state of mind when asking for guidance, we can be sure that our consistent efforts to seek knowledge of our Higher Power's will for us will be rewarded.

We should remember that Step Eleven asks us to pray *only* for the knowledge of God's will and the power to carry that out. Just as we opened our minds and avoided restricting our understanding of our Higher Power, we avoid placing limitations on what God's will for us can be. Though the temptation to pray for a particular result may be great, we must resist the urge to do so if we want to experience the rewards of the Eleventh Step. Praying for specific solutions to specific problems is not the answer.

For instance, at some time in our lives, we may feel unhappy but not know exactly what is causing such unhappiness. After spending a few minutes in prayer, seeking a specific solution to our unhappiness, we may suddenly get an idea that all our problems are caused by our boring job and demanding boss. We may even go to great lengths to convince ourselves that our idea was divinely inspired. We, as addicts, are subject to take such random thoughts and run with them, impulsively quitting our jobs. This scenario may seem extreme. Its point is that, by praying only for knowledge of God's will for us and the power to carry that out, we can avoid our former tendency to allow fleeting whims and superstition to dictate the course of our lives. Knowledge of our Higher Power's will does not usually come in a momentary blinding flash, but in a gradual awakening brought about by the continued practice of prayer and meditation.

Practicing the Eleventh Step involves a daily discipline of prayer and meditation. This discipline reinforces our commitment to recovery, to living a new way of life, and to developing further our relationship with our Higher Power. Through this daily practice, we begin to glimpse the limitless freedom we can be afforded through God's love. We have found that following such a discipline also results in a firm belief in our own right to happiness and peace of mind. We see that, regardless of the presence or absence of material success in our lives, we can be content. We can be happy and fulfilled with or without money, with or without a partner, with or without the approval of others. We've begun to see that God's will for us is the ability to live with dignity, to love ourselves and others, to laugh, and to find great joy and beauty in our surroundings. Our most heartfelt longings and dreams for our lives are coming true. These priceless gifts are no longer beyond our reach. They are, in fact, the very essence of God's will for us.

In our gratitude, we go beyond merely asking for the power to live up to God's plan for our own lives. We begin to seek out ways to be of service, to make a difference in the life of another addict, to carry the message of recovery. Our spiritual awakening has opened us up to spiritual contentment, unconditional love, and personal freedom. Knowing that we can only keep this precious gift by sharing it with others, we go on to Step Twelve.

STEP TWELVE

"Having had a spiritual awakening as a result of these steps, we tried to carry this message to addicts and to practice these principles in all our affairs."

In a sense, Step Twelve encompasses *all* the steps. We must make use of what we've learned in the previous eleven as we carry the message and practice the principles of recovery in all our affairs. Individually and collectively, each step has contributed to the extraordinary transformation which we know as a spiritual awakening.

Many of us have wondered how this spiritual awakening comes about. Does it happen all at once, or does it occur slowly over a long period of time? While there may be great variations within our experience about this awakening of the spirit, we all agree that it results from working the steps.

Our awakening has been progressive, beginning with a spark of awareness in the First Step. Before we admitted the truth about our addiction, we knew only the darkness of denial. But when we surrendered, acknowledging that we couldn't arrest our addiction or hope for a better life on our own, a ray of light broke through the darkness, beginning our spiritual awakening.

Though each individual's experience of a spiritual awakening varies, some experiences are so common as to be almost universal. Humility is one of these common factors. We first began to experience humility when we opened our minds to the possibility that a Power greater than ourselves existed. For some of us, this experience was so astounding that we received an almost physical jolt from the knowledge that we weren't alone in our struggle for recovery. Step Two allowed us our first glimpse of hope. That hope had an immediate and powerful effect on our despairing spirit, providing us with a reason to go on.

Our desire for something different prompted us to a deeper level of surrender in the Third Step. Not only did we admit that we couldn't control our addiction, we went on to recognize that our will and lives would be better left to the care of our Higher Power. Paradoxically, in this admission we found our greatest strength. As we worked the Third Step, we began to understand that we could tap the limitless resource of our Higher Power for everything needed to heal us spiritually.

This included the courage we knew we would need to work the Fourth Step. Many of us dreaded the process of self-appraisal called for in Step Four, despite the gentle assurances of our fellow NA members that we would find spiritual rewards in the process. Though we were afraid, we went forward, somehow believing in the experience of other recovering addicts. Once our inventory was completed, we no longer needed convincing. In the process, we had experienced spiritual growth for ourselves. Our spirits were strengthened by our emerging integrity. The shaping of values, so essential to our character, was just one of the positive results we found in the Fourth Step.

Unlike the admission we made in the First Step, which was made in desperation, the admission we made in Step Five was voluntary. This complete disclosure of our innermost selves, made without reservation, resulted in a breakthrough in our ability to accept ourselves and trust others. Our sponsor's acceptance and our Higher Power's unconditional love made it possible for us to judge ourselves less harshly. We developed a little more humility with the awareness of the exact nature of our wrongs. We began to understand that humility and self-loathing are incompatible and can't exist at the same time.

With our awareness of the exact nature of our wrongs—our character defects—and the humility inherent in that awareness, our desire to change increased dramatically as we worked Step Six. Though we may have experienced some apprehension about surrendering our character defects, we overcame our fears by drawing on the trust and faith we had developed in a loving God. Trust and faith, two important elements of a spiritual awakening, made it possible for us to become entirely ready to allow a Power greater than ourselves to work in our lives.

Consciously asking the God of our understanding to help us in Step Seven was an important development in the awakening of our spirit. That request was tangible evidence of how much we had changed spiritually. This was the point where many of us began to sense the enormous difference that our Higher Power could make in our lives. Because we had asked for and been granted some freedom from having to act on our shortcomings, we finally began to grasp what the miracle of recovery offers us.

Carried along by the promise of continued freedom in our lives, we proceeded, in Step Eight, to make ourselves aware of what we had done to others in our active addiction. Again, we saw how the spiritual preparation of the previous steps made it possible for us to withstand the pain and remorse of listing the people we had harmed. Our willingness to make amends to them all brought us further away from the grip of self-obsession. Our search for recovery was no longer focused on what we could get out of it for ourselves. We saw beyond the confines of our own lives, and our efforts in recovery began to be more generous. We developed the ability to feel empathy for others.

Once we had engaged in the process of making amends in the Ninth Step, we could see how it contributed to our spiritual growth. Our humility was enhanced by our newfound appreciation of others' feelings. Our self-esteem grew along with our increased capacity to forgive both ourselves and others. We were able to give of ourselves. Most of all, we gained freedom—freedom to live in the present and feel that we belonged in the world.

The discipline we practiced in the Tenth Step

ensured that we continued to breathe new life into our awakening spirits. We practiced ongoing adherence to our newfound values, thereby strengthening their importance in our lives. We saw that, by making our spiritual development our primary focus, other aspects of our lives would progress naturally as they were meant to all along.

Focusing our attention on our spiritual development brought us to the Eleventh Step. We had already become increasingly conscious of a powerful presence operating in our lives: a Power that could restore our sanity and remove our shortcomings. Through recognizing the love demonstrated by such actions, we started to better understand the loving nature of our Higher Power. The spiritual void we felt at the beginning of our recovery has been filled with gratitude, unconditional love, and a desire to be of service to God and others. Undeniably, we have experienced a spiritual awakening.

In order to cultivate this awakening, we have found it essential to express our gratitude and practice the principles of recovery in every area of our lives. However, this isn't something we do only to ensure that our own recovery continues. Narcotics Anonymous is not a selfish program. In fact, the spirit of the Twelfth Step is grounded in the principle of selfless service. Upholding this principle in our efforts to carry the message is of the utmost importance, both to our own spiritual state and to those to whom we are trying to carry the message.

Step Twelve has a paradoxical aspect in that the more we help others, the more we help ourselves. For instance, if we find ourselves troubled and our faith wavering, there are very few actions that have such an immediate uplifting effect on us as helping a newcomer. One small act of generosity can work wonders; our self-absorption diminishes and we end up with a better perspective on what previously seemed like overwhelming problems. Every time we tell someone else that Narcotics Anonymous works, we reinforce our belief in the program.

When being of service in Narcotics Anonymous, many of us have chosen to give back to the program in the same way we were helped when new. Some of us whose first contact with NA was through the area phoneline have found it rewarding to serve on the phoneline ourselves. Others have been drawn to hospitals and institutions service work because we first heard the message of NA in a jail or hospital. Whatever form of service we choose to be involved in, we do so with our primary purpose of carrying the message in mind.

Now we must ask ourselves, just what is "the message" we are trying to carry? Is it that we never have to use drugs again? Is it that, through recovery, we cease being likely candidates for jails, institutions, and an early death? Is it the hope that an addict, any addict, can recover from the disease of addiction? Well, it's all of this and more. The message we carry is that, by practicing the principles contained within the Twelve Steps, we have had a spiritual awakening. Whatever that means for each one of us is the message we carry to those seeking recovery.

The ways in which we carry the message are as varied as our members. There are, however, some basic guidelines that we, as a fellowship, have found to be helpful. First and foremost, we share our experience, strength, and hope. This means that we share our experience, not the theories we have heard from other sources. This also means that we share our *own* experience, not someone else's. It is not our job to tell someone seeking recovery where to work, who to live with, how to raise their children, or anything else outside the realm of our experience with recovery. Someone we are trying to help may have problems in these areas; we can help best not by managing that person's life, but by sharing our own experience in those areas.

Developing a personal style for carrying the message rests on a simple requirement: We must be ourselves. We each have a special, one-of-a-kind personality that is sure to be an attraction to many. Some of us have a sparkling sense of humor which may reach someone in despair. Some of us are especially warm and compassionate, able to reach an addict who has rarely been the recipient of kindness. Some of us have a remarkable talent for telling the truth, in no uncertain terms, to an addict literally dying to hear it. Some of us are a valuable asset on any service committee, while others do better working one-on-one with a

suffering addict. Whatever our own personality
makeup, we can be assured that when we sincerely
try to carry the message, we can reach the addict
seeking recovery.

Yet there are limits to what we can do to help
another addict. We cannot force anyone to stop using.
We cannot "give" someone the results of working the
steps, nor can we grow for them. We cannot magically
remove someone's loneliness or pain. Not only are
we powerless over our own addiction, we are
powerless over everyone else's. We can only carry the
message; we cannot determine who will receive it.

It is absolutely none of our business to decide who
is ready to hear the message of recovery and who is
not. Many of us have formed such a judgment about
an addict's desire for recovery and have been
mistaken. Multiple relapses do not necessarily signify
a lack of interest in recovery, nor does the "model
newcomer" demonstrate, without a doubt, a certainty
of "making it." It is our purpose and our privilege to
share the message of recovery unconditionally with
anyone expressing a desire to receive it.

The principle of unconditional love is expressed in
our attitude. Anyone who reaches out for help is
entitled to our compassion, our attention, and our
unconditional acceptance. Any addict, regardless of
clean time, should be able to pour out his or her pain
in an atmosphere free of judgment. Most of us have
found that we are able to feel great empathy for those
who suffer from our disease precisely because it is

our disease. Our empathy isn't abstract, nor is our understanding. Instead, it is born in shared experience. We greet each other with the recognition reserved for survivors of the same nearly fatal catastrophe. This shared experience, more than anything else, contributes to the atmosphere of unconditional love in our meetings.

Helping others is perhaps the highest aspiration of the human heart and something we have been entrusted with as a result of a Higher Power working in our lives. We would do well to remember to ask the God of our understanding to continue working through us in our efforts to carry the message. Diligently practicing the principles of recovery will ensure that the connection between ourselves and our Higher Power remains open and that our service to others is firmly rooted in spirituality.

Spirituality becomes a way of life for us as we live by the principles of recovery. The example of a life lived according to these principles is potentially the most powerful message we can carry. We don't need to wait until we're "on" the Second Step to practice the principle of open-mindedness. Courage and honesty have a place in our lives even when we aren't writing an inventory. Humility is always a desirable state, whether we are asking the God of our understanding to remove our shortcomings, conducting business with a co-worker, or talking to a friend.

To practice the principles of recovery in all our affairs is what we strive for. Both in and out of meetings, no matter who is involved, no matter how difficult it may seem, we make the principles of recovery the guides by which we live. Only through the practice of these principles in our daily life can we hope to achieve the spiritual growth necessary to maintain our reprieve from the disease of addiction. Though this may seem a lofty goal, we have found it attainable. Our gratitude for the gift of recovery becomes the underlying force in all we do, motivating us and weaving its way through our lives and the lives of those around us.

Even in silence, the voice of our gratitude does not go unheard. It speaks most clearly as we walk the path of recovery, selflessly giving to those we meet along the way. We venture forth on our spiritual journey, our lives enriched, our spirits awakened, and our horizons ever-expanding. The quintessential spirit that lies inside each one of us, the spark of life that was almost extinguished by our disease, has been renewed through working the Twelve Steps of Narcotics Anonymous. It is on the path paved with these steps that our future journey begins.

BOOK TWO
The Twelve Traditions

The traditions portion of It Works: How and Why serves as a resource for NA groups and the individual member. The book seeks to explore the spiritual principles within the traditions, engage members with the spirit—not the law—of the traditions, and provide a basis for thought and discussion about the traditions. This portion of the book is not meant to fulfill every need for every group or every member; rather, it is to be a book that will generate discussion and allow for local interpretation of the practical application of the principles contained in the traditions.

TRADITION ONE

"Our common welfare should come first; personal recovery depends on NA unity."

Narcotics Anonymous is more than just the first meeting we attend or the other NA meetings in our neighborhood. We are part of a much greater whole. Addicts apply the principles of Narcotics Anonymous in their personal recovery across town and around the world. Just as we learned in early recovery that we need each other to stay clean, we come to believe that all of us, every NA meeting and group, are interdependent. We share an equal membership in NA, and we all have an interest in maintaining the unity that underlies its common welfare. Unity is the spirit that joins thousands of members around the world in a spiritual fellowship that has the power to change lives.

One way to look at placing our common welfare first is to say that each of us is equally responsible for NA's well-being. In our recovery, we have found that living clean is very difficult without the support of other members. Our individual recovery depends on meetings that take place regularly, other recovering addicts who participate, and sponsors who share with us how to stay clean. Even members who can't get to meetings depend on the support of fellow addicts, maintaining contact with phone calls, letters, and NA loner groups. As each individual member relies on the support of the fellowship for survival, so NA's survival depends on its members.

Our First Tradition encourages not only our members but our groups to place our common welfare first. Most groups conduct most of their affairs on their own. In attending to the details of their week in, week out routines, autonomous NA groups may lose sight of the bigger picture. In the larger frame, each group is a strand in the supporting fabric of Narcotics Anonymous as a whole; without that fabric, there would be no NA. The importance of our unity encourages our groups to look beyond their own little worlds to the common needs of the worldwide NA Fellowship, placing the welfare of the whole before their own.

The relationship described in the First Tradition is reciprocal. Groups work together in a spirit of cooperation to ensure the survival of Narcotics Anonymous; in turn, those groups receive strength and support from every other group and all our services. The strength of our mutual commitment to NA creates the unity that binds us together in spite of all that might divide us. The common welfare of NA depends on the continued growth and well-being of the fellowship in every corner of the world.

Our shared commitment to recovery and to our common welfare gives us a personal stake in the unity of NA. In meetings, we find a new place to belong, new friends, and a hope for a better life. A feeling of care and concern grows between us and the group. We learn to treat others with kindness and respect and do what we can to support each other and our group.

Sometimes we comfort each other merely by being present; at other times, a phone call or letter simply to say hello can make a world of difference. Our relationships with other addicts are a source of strength in our personal recovery. We come to rely on meetings and on each other for that support. The unity we see in our meetings is an expression not only of our reliance on each other but our mutual reliance on spiritual principles and a Higher Power.

NA unity begins with our recognition of the therapeutic value of one addict helping another. We help each other in different ways. Sometimes we help each other one-on-one, as in sponsorship, or we may help each other by participating in the formation of new meetings to make NA accessible to more addicts. Many groups are formed when members of a more established group decide to start another meeting. Sharing the responsibility enhances our common welfare and creates unity among NA members who work together. Groups flourish with the loving support of addicts helping addicts. We strengthen our unity by participating in each other's recovery.

The unity described in our First Tradition is not the same thing as uniformity. Our membership is richly varied, made up of many addicts from widely differing backgrounds. These members bring with them a variety of ideas and talents. That diversity enriches the fellowship and gives rise to new and creative ways to reach addicts who need our help. Our purpose—to carry the message to the addict who still suffers—

allows room for everyone to serve. When we unite in support of this purpose, our differences need no longer detract from our common welfare. Working together for our mutual well-being is a significant source of unity in Narcotics Anonymous.

While we often think of unity as a feeling or a condition, unity doesn't just "happen." The unity underlying our common welfare requires personal commitment and responsible action. For example, when we accept personal responsibility for supporting our home group, we further NA unity and enhance the common welfare of the whole fellowship. Our commitment to unity strengthens our groups, allowing us to carry a message of hope. Meetings flourish in this atmosphere of hope. The fellowship grows and our common welfare increases as a result of our united efforts.

Communication goes a long way toward building and enhancing our common welfare. With an attitude of open-mindedness, we seek to understand other perspectives. Reports may tell us a lot about what's happening in other groups or areas, but our common welfare depends on more than just information. True communication involves an effort on our part to "listen" as we read or hear reports, seeking a better understanding of the needs and problems of both our own group and other groups, wherever they may be. Encouraging each member to speak openly from the heart enhances our ability to work together. Regular reports, thorough discussion, and active listening lead us to the kind of understanding that helps us find creative solutions that benefit us all.

Today's decisions may affect tomorrow's members. When we think of solutions to our current problems, it's not hard to consider the needs of our group, our area, our region, or even the worldwide fellowship. But it's also important to remember the "unseen members" in our discussions—the members yet to come. When we work to ensure the vitality of NA, we're not working just for ourselves but for those yet to join us.

The unity that supports our common welfare is created not only by working together but by playing together. The friendships we develop outside meetings strengthen NA unity. Fellowship activities provide opportunities for us to relax, socialize with each other, and have fun. Conventions, dinners, and holiday celebrations give us a chance to celebrate our recovery while practicing social skills. Picnics, dances, and sports days, for example, often allow our families to participate, too. We strengthen our sense of community when we share more than just meeting time. Stronger relationships develop as we become more involved in each other's lives. The care and understanding born of these relationships are strong threads in the fabric of NA unity.

Applying spiritual principles

In the Twelve Steps of NA, we learn to apply principles to better our lives. Moved by the miracle of personal recovery, we reach out to share that miracle with others. This is the essence of being of service in NA. In supporting our unity, we first apply principles to guide our own behavior. As groups, we use the same principles for guidance. That guidance engenders a sense of unity that strengthens our ability to reach out to others, enhancing our common welfare. Some of the principles that seem particularly important to unity include surrender and acceptance, commitment, selflessness, love, and anonymity. As we practice these principles, we will find others that strengthen unity as well.

Surrender and acceptance open the door to unity. As our trust in a Higher Power grows, it gets easier to let go of our personal desires and stop fighting for what we want. With an attitude of surrender, working together in a group becomes easier. Tradition One presents a picture of addicts working together worldwide to support each other's recovery. We try to remember this goal in all our actions, as individuals or as groups. If we find that our personal desires or the aims of our group conflict with that ideal, unity asks us to surrender our own desires and accept guidance that enhances the greater good of Narcotics Anonymous. Only by deciding to be part of that whole can we support the unity so essential to our personal survival.

Commitment is another essential ingredient in unity. Personal commitment to our shared sense of purpose is one of the ties that bind us together. When we know that we belong in NA, and when we make a commitment to stay, we become a part of the greater whole. Our sense of belonging is closely related to our degree of commitment to recovery in NA. As groups, the combined strength of that commitment is a powerful force in serving others. With that strong commitment, we are able to carry the message of hope that will support us all in our recovery.

Commitment is a decision supported by our belief in NA as a way of life. Regular meeting attendance is one of the ways in which we live out that belief. Greeting newcomers as they arrive or giving our telephone number to someone who needs help also reflects our decision. Sponsorship, sharing in meetings, setting up chairs before a meeting—all these are ways in which we express our commitment. Each member finds a level of service that fits comfortably into a balanced program of recovery.

Selflessness is another indispensable element in unity. The principles we learn in the steps help us let go of our selfishness and lovingly serve the needs of others. To keep our groups healthy, we place the needs of our group ahead of our own personal desires. The same principle applies to our affairs as a group. Setting aside what we may want as a group, we think about the needs of the fellowship and seek ways to support our common good. Our ability to survive as a fellowship and to reach others depends on our unity.

Love is a principle that is expressed in the practice of goodwill toward one another. We contribute to unity in our meetings by exercising loving care in the way we speak and the way we treat one another. We try to share our experience, strength, and hope in a way which demonstrates that recovery is available in Narcotics Anonymous. An atmosphere of love and care in our meetings helps members feel comfortable and safe. The love we show each other attracts newcomers and strengthens us all, fueling our sense of unity and common welfare.

Anonymity, the spiritual foundation of our traditions, supports NA unity as well. When we apply anonymity to the First Tradition, we overlook the differences that would separate us. In the context of unity, anonymity means that the message of recovery is for every addict who wants it. We learn to set aside our prejudices and focus on our common identity as addicts. Each of us has an equal right to and responsibility for the well-being of Narcotics Anonymous.

Just as anonymity is the *spiritual* foundation of our traditions, the unity spoken of in the First Tradition is the *practical* foundation on which we may build strong and successful groups. Each succeeding tradition builds upon the strength of our unity as a fellowship, recalling the vital importance of the common welfare to each individual member and group. With unity as our practical foundation, we find that our relationship with one another is more important than any issue that may arise to divide us. No problem or disagreement is more significant than our need for each other's support. The fundamental importance of our common welfare strengthens our understanding of all the other traditions. Many questions can be answered simply by determining how the action we contemplate will affect the unity of the fellowship. Will it serve to divide us, or will it bring us closer together?

Unity is the spirit that joins members around the world in a spiritual fellowship that has the power to change lives. By striving to see beyond our individual ideas and the interests of our own group, we come to understand that the common welfare of all NA must come first. Through our trust in a loving Higher Power, we find the strength to work together toward our shared goal of recovery from addiction. In the unity that grows in trust, we are ready to work together for our common good.

TRADITION TWO

*"For our group purpose there is but one
ultimate authority—a loving God as He may
express Himself in our group conscience.
Our leaders are but trusted servants;
they do not govern."*

Tradition Two builds on the practical foundation of Tradition One. We begin with unity, founded on the strength of our commitment to recovery in Narcotics Anonymous. Our commitment is reflected in service that builds our common welfare: supporting a meeting, sharing with other members, sponsorship, any of the ways in which we reach out to other addicts. As groups, too, our purpose is to serve, to carry the message. Everything we do in service to NA is related to that purpose. Without direction, however, our services might lack consistency. To guide us in serving others, we seek direction from a Higher Power.

Personal service arises from the application of principles. Ideally, personal service is founded in a relationship with the same Higher Power that guides our personal recovery. This Higher Power also guides the various elements of our fellowship. Our direction in service comes from a God of our understanding, whether we serve as individuals, as a group, or as a service board or committee. Whenever we come together, we seek the presence and guidance of this loving Higher Power. This direction then guides us through all our actions.

Everybody has opinions on how to serve more effectively. When we each propose a different plan for any course of action, how do we choose among them? Who has the final say in our discussions? Our answer is that a loving God, the source of our unity, has the final say—the same Higher Power that guides our personal recovery.

If we are to find guidance from an ultimate authority, we need to find means of hearing that guidance together. The mechanism we use is group conscience. The success of the group conscience process depends on our willingness as individuals to seek guidance from a Higher Power on a personal level. We then bring that willingness into the group setting.

Something happens when we practice the steps and learn to apply principles in our individual lives. We develop an awareness of our behavior and its effects on ourselves and others. In other words, we develop a conscience. This conscience is a reflection of our relationship with a Higher Power. It reflects the guidance we receive from the God of our understanding and our commitment to follow that guidance. Whenever we come together in our groups, a similar process may occur: A collective conscience develops. That conscience reflects the relationship of our members to a loving Higher Power. When consulted regularly, that collective conscience guides us in fulfilling our primary purpose while preserving our unity and common welfare.

Group conscience can be thought of in much the same way as personal conscience. Group conscience reflects a collective awareness of, understanding of, and surrender to spiritual principles. The conscience of a group takes shape and is revealed when its members take the time to talk with each other about their personal needs, the needs of that group, and the needs of NA as a whole. Each member draws upon his or her relationship with a Higher Power when sharing with the group. As members listen carefully to each other and consult their personal understanding of a loving God, something happens: Solutions to problems become apparent, solutions that take into consideration the needs of everyone concerned. In developing a group conscience, a clear mutual understanding or consensus arises. Based upon the understanding gained by sharing group conscience, a group may move on to a vote in order to make decisions. In the best of circumstances, however, the group continues discussion until it reaches unanimity. The resulting solution may be so obvious that no vote is needed.

Group conscience is not fixed and inflexible. We know that personal conscience changes as an individual's relationship with a Higher Power grows and strengthens. In the same way, the conscience of a group evolves as its members mature in recovery, new members arrive, and the group's situation changes.

Group conscience is a process that may work differently under differing circumstances. It's not reasonable to expect that today's solution to one group's needs will always be sufficient for every group; in fact, that solution may not even apply to the same group at a different time. The principles involved in group conscience are always the same, but the times and conditions our conscience guides us through are constantly changing, requiring our conscience to tell us different things in different settings. It's important for us to continue cultivating our group conscience, seeking the guidance of a loving Higher Power whenever a question arises.

A surrender to group conscience means we allow our fellowship to be shaped by a loving Higher Power. We are tempted sometimes to take control of the daily affairs of our group, our service board, or our committee, believing that our great concern for the fellowship's welfare could never lead us astray. However, as we become more trusting, we realize that the group is directed by a loving Higher Power. Our reliance on that Higher Power is demonstrated by our willingness to carry out the direction expressed in our group conscience, believing that all will be well.

Any group, board, or committee can become bogged down in disagreement or sidetracked by seemingly insurmountable problems. In these situations, it's important to focus our attention on the principles of the program and the solutions they point toward, not on our problems. Agreement is reached when we step out of the way and allow a loving Higher Power to direct us.

Only when we listen for the direction of a Higher Power are we able to hear it. The conscience of a group is most clearly expressed when every member is considered an equal. A Higher Power works through all of us, regardless of clean time or experience. Group conscience always exists, but we are not always willing or able to hear it or allow its expression. Hearing group conscience may take time and patience. A flexible approach invites a loving Higher Power into our group conscience process.

In our personal recovery, our thoughts and actions change as we stay clean and grow spiritually. We don't get better overnight, and sometimes our growth is sporadic and uneven. This same pattern of growth and maturation also occurs in our fellowship. As our groups grow and evolve, our resources change and so do our needs. Groups may change trusted servants, meeting format, or location, depending on their resources and their needs; service committees may expand their subcommittees, reach out into new territories, or combine their efforts with other committees. These changes may not always feel like progress. Just as our personal recovery doesn't always develop in an orderly fashion, our fellowship doesn't always evolve as we would expect. As groups and committees go through this growing process, their collective conscience often evolves as well. Changes in the group conscience are not a cause for alarm, merely part of the growing process.

When a group or committee has sought direction from a loving Higher Power, it may ask some of its members to help carry out that direction. When we ask members to serve, we don't set them apart as being somehow better than the rest of us. Leadership in NA is a service, not a class of membership. For this reason, we call our leaders *trusted servants*.

When we choose a member to serve us in some capacity, we exercise mutual trust. We trust the conscience that influenced our selection since it reflects our collective relationship with a loving Higher Power. We extend that trust to the members we have selected to serve. We have faith that they will apply principles in their actions, seek and share the most complete information available, and work to further the group's well-being and our fellowship's common welfare. The relationship of trusted servants to the group is reciprocal: Members chosen to serve are asked to do so with dedication and fidelity, and those who've chosen them are responsible to support their servants.

When we are asked to serve, we understand that we are responsible to a loving Higher Power as expressed in the group conscience. We acknowledge this responsibility when we approach service with a selfless and loving attitude. The principles embodied in the traditions apply to all our actions. We can look to our individual conscience as well as the collective conscience for guidance in all we must do in fulfilling our responsibilities.

This connection with the group conscience is enhanced when, as trusted servants, we carry a continuous flow of information that is honest and open; it is further strengthened when we seek to serve, not to govern. We help form the conscience of our group or committee, through the direction of a Higher Power, by presenting a complete and unbiased stream of information. The ideas and direction of the group, then, are conveyed in our representation of that conscience.

Our trusted servants lead us best when they lead by personal example. Ideally, we choose them for the principles of recovery we see at work in their lives. We encourage our trusted servants to remain open to new ideas, to become knowledgeable about all aspects of service in NA, and to continue to seek personal recovery. All of these attributes are essential to their ability to serve us well.

Applying spiritual principles

We noted earlier in this chapter that personal service arises from the practice of principles. By applying these principles, we learn to seek direction. We talk to our sponsor, share with our NA friends, and listen for a Higher Power's guidance. Some of the principles that seem to be important in Tradition Two include surrender, faith, humility, open-mindedness, integrity, and anonymity.

We begin with surrender to our ultimate authority, the God of our understanding, with whom we have developed a personal relationship. In this case, we surrender to the direction of that Higher Power as it is revealed in our group conscience. We renew our commitment to the common welfare of NA when we place the needs of the fellowship ahead of our own desires.

Faith is our reliance on a loving Higher Power put into action. The application of this spiritual principle lets us surrender to the group conscience with hope instead of fear. It is a constant reminder that our direction comes from a Power greater than our own. Faith demands courage, since we often practice an active demonstration of faith in spite of our anxiety. Our faith is strengthened through the experience of seeing a loving Higher Power work in our fellowship.

Humility in practice is the honest assessment of our strengths and weaknesses. That kind of assessment is a necessary ingredient in our willingness to surrender. Humility prepares us to set aside our personal wishes so that we can effectively serve our fellowship. We look to humility, first, to remind us that we aren't personally capable of guiding the affairs of Narcotics Anonymous. We are reminded of our source of strength: a loving Higher Power.

By practicing humility in our efforts to serve, we make room for open-mindedness. We remember that, just as we need the experience of other addicts to recover, so do we need their direction and ideas in order to serve. We learn to actively cultivate our listening skills, using our ears more than our mouths in conversation. When we are open-minded, we hear and accept solutions offered by others in the development of group conscience. Application of this principle teaches us to set aside our prejudices in order to work with others. By practicing open-mindedness, we nurture an attitude of goodwill toward others and become willing to serve with our common good in mind. Only with an open mind can we recognize the guidance of a loving Higher Power.

Integrity is the consistent application of spiritual principles, no matter what the circumstances. Leaders who demonstrate this quality inspire our trust. We serve best when we display an honest respect for the trust placed in us by others. Fidelity and devotion to that trust reflect the personal integrity of our servants. When we choose members to serve us, we often look for integrity as a sign that they are trustworthy.

The spiritual principle of anonymity reminds us that we are all equal in Narcotics Anonymous. No one member or group has a monopoly on the knowledge of a Higher Power's will. We practice anonymity by offering our love, attention, and respect to everyone, regardless of our personal feelings toward any individual. Every member has a part in the development of group conscience. We are all equal in the expression of a conscious contact with a Higher Power of our understanding.

Tradition Two offers guidance for our relationships with others. A loving Higher Power is the source of direction for NA as a whole. This Higher Power is also the source of the principles that we apply when we serve. We can use these principles when we seek direction as individuals, groups, service boards, or committees.

Service is for those we serve. Our best talent in service is the ability to reach other addicts, offer identification and welcome, greet the addict walking in the door for the first time, and help ensure that newcomers return again and again. Any one of us is capable of offering that service. With the guidance of a loving Higher Power, we become better able to help others.

Service to the Fellowship of Narcotics Anonymous has its own rewards. When we practice spiritual principles in our daily lives, a stronger relationship with our Higher Power develops. Our relationship with our group and the fellowship grows stronger, too. Service in NA is a learning experience that allows us personal growth. We begin to look beyond our own interests, setting aside our self-centered view of life in order to better serve the whole. We benefit spiritually in return for our unselfish service.

TRADITION THREE

"The only requirement for membership is a
desire to stop using."

Narcotics Anonymous offers recovery to addicts around the world. We focus on the disease of addiction rather than any particular drug. Our message is broad enough to attract addicts from any social class or nationality. When new members come to meetings, our sole interest is in their desire for freedom from active addiction and how we can be of help.

The Third Tradition helps NA offer recovery to so many addicts by freeing us from having to make judgments about prospective members. It eliminates the need for membership committees or applications. We are not asked to make decisions about anyone's fitness for recovery. Since the only requirement for membership is a desire to stop using, we as members have no reason to judge each other.

Desire is not a measurable commodity. It lives in the heart of each individual member. Because we can't judge the sole requirement for membership, we are encouraged to open wide the doors of our meetings to any addict who wishes to join. We are asked to extend to others the care and concern that helped each of us find a sense of belonging. The Third Tradition helps NA grow by encouraging us to welcome others.

Membership is a personal decision reached by each individual. We can do a lot to allow addicts the freedom to make that decision and reaffirm their commitment to recovery. We can help them feel comfortable in our groups by greeting them at the door, sharing with other addicts before or after the meeting, and exchanging telephone numbers. We try to make sure that any addict who attends our meeting is not turned away. To the extent that it's possible, we choose the most accessible location for our meetings. We may choose a format that reflects an invitational tone. Most of all, we encourage every addict to keep coming back.

The strength of any member's desire is not necessarily connected to any outside circumstance. What makes one addict stay clean while another returns to using? No one of us can judge who will stay to recover and who will return to active addiction. There are no guarantees based on types of drugs used or using history. We cannot predict a higher success rate for addicts of a certain age, or those who used for a certain number of years, or women over men, or any other external factor. Just as we are not capable of measuring another's desire to stay clean, neither are we equipped to decide who should join. We are free to offer welcome instead of judgment.

We look for ways to help instead of judge. Our task is to fan the flame of desire, not dampen it. Any addict who walks into a meeting, even a using addict, displays a level of willingness that cannot be discounted. While maintaining an emphasis on the importance of total abstinence, still-using addicts are welcomed into our meetings with special encouragement to keep coming back. Many recovering addicts do not have access to regular meetings because of incarceration, geography, physical disability, or employment. These addicts are members in every respect as long as they have the desire to stop using, and they are entitled to the same consideration and support as any other member. Addicts attend their first meeting for many reasons. Our motives for coming to NA aren't particularly important. The desire to stop using may not be clearly realized; it may be no more than a subtle yearning for relief from pain. But that yearning often drives us to seek solutions we might otherwise never consider. Often the experience of hearing other addicts share about recovery will ignite the desire to stop using. Others come to a meeting, hear the message, and return to active addiction. Those who return to meetings after relapse often say their desire to stop using was born from the pain of relapse. We come to NA for many reasons, but we stay to recover when we find and keep the desire to stop using.

The group is not the jury of desire. We cannot measure or arbitrate willingness. Any addict's willingness to come to a meeting ought to be a sufficient indication of desire. It may take a while for an addict to find the desire that will keep her or him in Narcotics Anonymous. No addict should be denied an opportunity to stay long enough to develop that desire. We can nurture that desire with loving acceptance.

The wording of the Third Tradition reflects the broad focus of our First Step. It's written simply enough to include addicts of all countries and cultures, no matter what drugs they used. Before finding recovery in NA, many addicts don't think that alcohol is a problem. Others abuse prescription medication, thinking that "legal" drugs are okay. Because of the wording of this tradition, we are able to attract and welcome addicts who might think they didn't use the "right" drugs to qualify for membership in NA. Each addict should be allowed to decide if NA is the answer for him or herself. We cannot make the decision for others.

Although the Third Tradition is written simply, we know that when it talks about "a desire to stop using," it means using *drugs*. We understand that NA is a program of recovery for drug addicts. Although *addiction* takes on a broader meaning for many of us as we continue in recovery, it's important to remember that we first came to NA because of our drug problems. If new members are to feel that they belong in NA, they need to hear something they can identify with. They find that identification in the fellowship of recovering addicts in Narcotics Anonymous.

Many of us know when we walk into our first meeting that we're addicts. It's not something we have to decide; it's just a fact of life. Membership, however, means more than just being an addict; it means making a decision. If we identify with what we hear in NA and relate with the people we meet, we will want what NA offers. So long as we have a desire to stop using, we are free to make the decision to join Narcotics Anonymous. Then, once we've made that decision, we need to follow it with a commitment to the principles of NA. With that commitment, we set ourselves squarely on the road of recovery.

Applying spiritual principles

The Third Tradition encourages freedom from judgment. It leads us on the path of service toward an attitude of helpfulness, acceptance, and unconditional love. As we've seen in the previous traditions, our path of service arises from the application of principles. Some of the principles that support this tradition include tolerance, compassion, anonymity, and humility.

Tolerance reminds us that judgment is not our task. The disease of addiction does not exclude anyone. NA, likewise, cannot exclude any addict who desires to stop using. We learn to be tolerant of addicts from different backgrounds than ours, remembering that we are not better than any other addict in a meeting.

Addiction is a deadly disease. We know that addicts who don't find recovery can expect nothing better than jails, institutions, and death. Refusing admission to any addict, even one who comes merely out of curiosity, may be a death sentence for that addict. We learn to practice tolerance of addicts who don't look like us, think like us, or share like us. We teach by example. Pressuring new members to talk or act like we do may send them back to the streets. It certainly denies them the right to recover and learn in their own way.

Compassion lends kindness to all our efforts in service to others. With compassion as the foundation of our actions, we learn to support members through any difficulties they may experience. All too often, we are quick to judge the quality of another's recovery or willingness. Tradition Three asks us to set aside our self-righteousness. Because the only requirement for membership is a quality we cannot measure, the right to judge another's desire is denied us. Our attitude ought to be one of loving acceptance toward *all* addicts, regardless of any other problems they may experience. Generous application of compassion is more therapeutic to the suffering addict than a free application of judgment.

Humility reminds us that we are not God; we cannot predict another's readiness to hear the message. We try to remember our own fear and confusion in our first meeting. We need each other's help and encouragement, not criticism or rejection. Our awareness of our own shortcomings, exercised in humility, helps us remember this. The self-acceptance that often accompanies humility makes us reluctant to judge others harshly.

Anonymity is the principle that supports the openness of our groups and our freedom to welcome everyone as equals. NA has no classes of membership and no second-class members. The common denominator in NA is the disease of addiction. We are all equally subject to its devastation. We share an equal right to recovery.

The practice of anonymity ensures the integrity of Tradition Three. In the spirit of anonymity, we remember that no individual member or group is more important than the message we carry. The single requirement for membership helps ensure that no addict need die without having a chance to recover. We celebrate our equality and the freedom we share by welcoming any addict who has the desire to stop using.

Tradition Three spells freedom for the members of NA. It sets the sole requirement for membership in the heart of each individual member. We don't have to decide for anyone else. We don't have to expend time and energy on deciding who should stay or who we should help. Instead, we are free to extend loving assistance to anyone who walks into a meeting desiring freedom from addiction.

TRADITION FOUR

"Each group should be autonomous, except in matters affecting other groups or NA as a whole."

NA groups have a great deal of freedom. We've already seen in Tradition Three that groups are free of any need to screen their members or set requirements for membership. Our NA groups are free to offer recovery to any addict. The Fourth Tradition enhances that freedom, allowing the rich diversity of our varied experience to help us serve.

Freedom can be exhilarating. Many of us have little experience with freedom of any sort. Our lives in active addiction often seemed more like slavery. When we first experience the freedom of recovery, we may find it overwhelming. Through working the steps, we learn that with freedom comes responsibility. In recovery, we become responsible for ourselves. As we accept that responsibility, we see how the Fourth Tradition encourages us to act responsibly as groups and as a fellowship.

NA groups are vehicles for the message of recovery. In the strength of the personal commitment group members make to one another, a group character forms. As this group character grows and evolves, the group finds ways in which it can do what no other group in town may be doing. The members of each group design a blueprint for meetings that reflect that particular group's personality.

Group autonomy gives groups the creative freedom to find individual ways to carry the message. NA is made up of a vastly diverse assortment of addicts joined together by the strength of their mutual commitment to recovery. We speak many different languages and live in differing cultures; one type of meeting will not appeal to every addict who comes to Narcotics Anonymous. In order to reach every addict who may need our help and support the recovery of every member, groups have the freedom to vary their format and other meeting characteristics. Each group has the freedom to pursue our primary purpose in the manner it feels will work best.

Every group has a niche to fill, both in the fellowship as a whole and in the local NA community. As a fellowship, our ability to reach still-using addicts is tied to our willingness to offer meetings that are accessible and attractive to those addicts. With the creative freedom offered by autonomy, we are encouraged to seek the particular role that meets the needs of both the NA community and our own group. We are free to make each group the very best it can be. The vitality of Narcotics Anonymous is enhanced by each group's willingness to find its niche and fill it.

Creative freedom challenges the groups to be strong and responsible. Members may support many meetings with their attendance, but most make a commitment to support one group in particular. Members grow in their personal recovery when they take responsibility for their lives. In the same way, groups grow and become stronger when their members take collective responsibility for maintaining their meetings. Groups reflect the responsibility and commitment of their members.

One of the most common ways in which groups express their autonomy is in the choice of meeting format. Most NA communities will offer a number of different types of meetings, from speaker meetings to step studies to topic discussions or any other format or combination of formats that meets the needs of local members. Some meetings will be open to the public, while others will be for addicts only. Larger communities may offer several different types of meetings each night. Some addicts will hear the message of recovery better in one type of meeting, while others prefer another format. An NA community that offers a variety of meetings is more likely to reach a broad cross-section of addicts. In a spirit of cooperation, we try to respect the autonomy of other groups by allowing them the freedom to carry the message in whatever manner seems best to them.

In the spirit of autonomy, many groups hold meetings that appeal to members with similar needs. The freedom from judgment expressed in the Third Tradition is aimed at helping any addict, anywhere, feel comfortable in NA. No matter how a group structures its meetings, all NA groups are encouraged to keep the focus of their meetings on recovery from the disease of addiction. As long as a group observes the Twelve Traditions and espouses the Twelve Steps of NA in its meetings, it may consider them Narcotics Anonymous meetings.

Sometimes it's hard to know what affects NA as a whole. The Fourth Tradition offers a way to balance the freedom of autonomy with our responsibility to preserve NA unity. We are challenged in Tradition Four to apply autonomy in ways that will enhance the growth and vitality of NA. Autonomy encourages groups to become strong and lively but also reminds them that they are a vital part of a greater whole: the Fellowship of Narcotics Anonymous. We consider our common welfare when we make decisions in our groups.

Since most groups are not directly connected with each other, we might think that whatever happens in our meetings has no effect on anyone else. When we consider who is affected by our group, we have to look at other groups, the addict yet to come, the newcomer, and the neighborhood in which we hold our meetings. We have an effect on other groups or NA as a whole if we're not recognizable as an NA meeting. It helps to remember what we needed to hear when we were new: hope for recovery from drug addiction. Addicts first coming to NA often look closely for differences, hoping that somehow they won't fit in. It's not difficult to alienate an addict. It's important to think about the message we send to newcomers in our meetings. Thoughtful consideration of our primary purpose may help ensure that meetings will be available for those addicts yet to come.

It's also important to consider how we're viewed by society. When NA meetings first began in many places, it was illegal for addicts to meet under any circumstances. Even where meetings are legal, the public often views groups of addicts with alarm. Until NA has established a good public reputation, it may be difficult for addicts to find meeting places. If our behavior as NA members is still destructive and selfish, we will once again have difficulty meeting openly. We help protect our reputation as a fellowship when we use our meeting facilities with respect, keeping them clean and in good repair. We should take care to act like good neighbors, conducting ourselves respectfully. Even something as simple as the name a group chooses may reflect on NA as a whole. If the public reputation of Narcotics Anonymous is somehow impaired, addicts may die.

Autonomy does not relieve groups of their obligation to observe and apply the spiritual principles embodied in the traditions. Careful consideration of the group's observation of the Fourth Tradition often takes the form of a group inventory, helping members gauge their success at carrying the message and reaching addicts in their neighborhood. At the same time, groups can examine their part in contributing to the unity of NA as a whole. The Fourth Tradition guides us away from self-centeredness by giving us the freedom to act responsibly as groups.

Applying spiritual principles

The Fourth Tradition helps groups achieve a balance between independence and responsibility. This mirrors the freedom of the individual recovering member and the responsibility which supports that freedom. Together with open-mindedness, unity, and anonymity, these principles help protect NA as a whole when applied in our group affairs.

While autonomy gives us certain freedoms, it also implies responsibility for our actions and for the continued well-being of NA. As groups, we exercise our responsibility to the fellowship by taking inventory of our behavior and how we hold meetings. Our group exercises its autonomy in a responsible way when it takes care to consider the common welfare of the fellowship as a whole before it acts.

Open-mindedness is essential if we are to use autonomy to help NA grow. With an open-minded attitude, we are more receptive to new ways of reaching addicts. We learn to find and fill our niche in the NA community. We encourage each member of the group to contribute thoughts and ideas. Our attitude of open-mindedness helps us remember that each group is part of a greater whole. Acknowledging that we are part of something bigger than ourselves prompts us to look at still more new ideas. Our diversity can enrich us only when we are open to its richness.

Remembering our part in the greater whole, we consider unity when we think about applying the

Fourth Tradition. Any decision that we make as an autonomous group ought to be founded first in our common welfare. Although we are autonomous, we may offer loving support to other groups by attending their meetings or offering other help. NA meetings thrive when groups look beyond their immediate needs to offer help to each other.

Love is the principle that guides us to see NA as a greater whole. This impacts our responsibility as autonomous groups. Our group's autonomous decisions, based on our love for NA, will serve to strengthen our efforts to serve others. Love encourages us to reach out to other members and other groups, finding ways to cooperate with them in carrying the message of recovery.

Anonymity applied to the Fourth Tradition reminds us that each group has an equal place in the Fellowship of NA. Larger groups are not more important than smaller groups; older groups are not "better" than newer groups. While all groups have the freedom to apply principles in whatever ways seem best to them, those same principles make each group an equal partner in recovery. Each group bears an equal responsibility in the work and in the reputation of NA.

Autonomy in NA gives groups the freedom to act on their own to establish an atmosphere of recovery, serve their members, and fulfill our primary purpose. The responsibility that balances our autonomy reflects the principles expressed in the first three traditions. Preserving the unity of the NA Fellowship comes first.

Next, we seek direction from a loving Higher Power. Then, we hold meetings that welcome everyone with a desire to stop using.

Healthy, vital groups are essential to the growth of Narcotics Anonymous. Groups provide a place where we can offer our most basic service: one addict reaching out to another with the message of recovery. Without our autonomous groups, we would be unable to fulfill our primary purpose.

TRADITION FIVE

"Each group has but one primary purpose—
to carry the message to the addict who
still suffers."

Our primary purpose is at the heart of our service. With guidance from a loving Higher Power and a clear focus on this purpose, NA groups become a channel for the healing power of recovery. Narcotics Anonymous exists to help addicts find freedom from active addiction. If we were to espouse other ideas or pursue other goals, our focus would be blurred and our energies diminished. The Fifth Tradition asks us to practice integrity by keeping our purpose foremost.

Tradition Five helps our groups fulfill the fundamental reason for their existence: to carry the message to the addict who still suffers. As we learned in the Fourth Tradition, NA groups are free to find new and different ways of presenting meetings. This freedom is important; it protects and encourages diversity, letting us reach addicts by many means. In this autonomy, each group develops a character of its own. The character of the group is not its purpose, however. The message we carry is not our group personality but the message of Narcotics Anonymous—the principles of recovery.

What is the message that we are asked to carry? Groups carry the message of NA: hope and freedom from active addiction. This message may be voiced in many ways. Sometimes we simply share that if we won't use any drugs, we won't get loaded. Other members share that they have found satisfying, productive lives in recovery. Sometimes the message we share is that, even though life may be painful, we can stay clean. The spiritual awakening we experience when we work the steps is also our message. When addicts experience the message of recovery, we find healing from our suffering, no matter what the cause. We can live drug-free and establish new lives. That is our message: that an addict, any addict, can stop using drugs, lose the desire to use, and find a new way to live.

The groups' focus on carrying the message is so important to the survival of NA that it is called our primary purpose. That means it is the most important thing we do. Nothing ought to take precedence over it. This is the most basic guideline by which groups may examine their motives and their actions.

There are many ways in which groups can further our primary purpose. Generally speaking, group members start by creating an atmosphere of recovery in their meetings. This includes extending a welcome to every addict who attends. Stable meetings that start on time carry a message of recovery. Effective meeting formats keep the primary purpose in focus and encourage members to participate in a way that expresses recovery. We lead by example, sharing experience instead of advice. Group members help further our purpose when they take personal responsibility for keeping the meeting recovery-oriented. All of our actions convey a message, and Tradition Five reminds us to make it a message of recovery.

There are many distracting influences that can divert us from our primary purpose. For instance, our groups may be tempted to use meeting time to discuss their business and finances or talk about some controversy. As individual members, we can get caught up in socializing with our friends, ignoring another addict who may be in pain and needs our encouragement. But each time our focus is diverted from our primary purpose, the addict seeking recovery loses out.

Other influences can distort our group's focus on its primary purpose. From the money members contribute, our groups pay rent on their meeting space, buy literature and supplies, conduct activities, and support NA services. All of these can either help further our primary purpose or distract us from our focus. Some groups seek to outdo others with luxurious meeting spaces, extravagant refreshments, huge supplies of literature, and elaborate activities. When we do this, our focus is distracted away from our primary purpose and onto money, property, and prestige. We should try to establish a reputation for carrying the message—nothing more, nothing less. Money, literature, and meeting space are tools we can use to help us carry the message; however, they should serve us, not rule us.

The groups can provide many services to carry the message. Our primary service is the NA meeting, where addicts share their recovery directly with one another. Additional services like phonelines, public information work, and H&I panels also help carry the message. In rural areas and newer NA communities, groups are sometimes the only source of such services. However, most groups find they cannot maintain their focus on their recovery meetings and also carry out other services. For this reason, groups usually assign responsibility for such services to their area committees. That way, groups reserve their time and energy for carrying the message directly to the addict who still suffers.

Because carrying the message is so important, many groups take inventory periodically to help ensure that our primary purpose is still in focus. The Twelve Traditions may be used as an outline for a group inventory. Some groups use a specific set of inventory questions, such as: How well are we carrying the message of recovery? Are there addicts our group isn't reaching? How can we make our meetings more accessible? What can we do to make new members feel more at home? Has the atmosphere of recovery diminished? Would a change in our meeting format strengthen that atmosphere?

Considering the needs of the larger NA community may lead to other changes. For instance, if there are no step meetings in one town, a group may consider having meetings that focus on the steps. There are many ways to carry the message and meet the needs of both the group and the NA community.

There is a power that works through this program. We tap this power when we practice the Twelfth Step as individuals, carrying the message to other addicts. When groups carry the message, the impact of the Twelfth Step is greatly multiplied. Even more impressive than sheer numbers of recovering addicts is the unity of purpose and the atmosphere of recovery found in meetings—a spiritual power. The evidence of that power in the group is hard to deny. It is a power we can draw on between meetings to stay clean.

Tradition Five focuses the group's priority on carrying the message. Members can do many things to further our primary purpose. For example, we show our care and our willingness to help by taking turns greeting people at the door, preparing lists of telephone numbers to distribute, or offering packets of literature to newcomers. When members come together as a group to undertake the task of carrying the message, they offer an attractive picture of recovery in action.

Many meetings are structured to carry the message to our newest members. These new members often need more encouragement to stay, more answers to their questions, more of our love and care. But the newest members are not the only addicts who need the message of recovery. The still-suffering addict with whom we share our hope may be any one of us, regardless of clean time. Tradition Five is not limited to helping newcomers. The message of recovery is for all of us.

Applying spiritual principles

The Fifth Tradition complements the Twelfth Step: It asks *groups* to carry the message to addicts. As individuals, we are asked in the steps to apply principles in all our affairs; this is also important in our actions as groups. Some of the principles we have applied to help us observe the Fifth Tradition include integrity, responsibility, unity, and anonymity.

Integrity, or fidelity to the principles embodied in the Twelve Traditions, is demonstrated when groups carry the NA message of recovery. Many of our members have much to offer on a variety of subjects, but our fellowship has its own special message: freedom from active addiction through practice of NA's Twelve Steps and the support of the fellowship of recovering addicts. Groups demonstrate this when they offer vigorous, conscious support for addicts seeking to work the NA program. When groups conscientiously cultivate this kind of integrity, their meetings further our primary purpose.

The Fifth Tradition gives our groups a great responsibility: to maintain our fellowship's primary purpose. Each group is responsible to become as effective a vehicle for carrying the NA message as it can be. Allowing our groups to lose sight of our primary purpose may deprive an addict of a chance to hear our message of hope. Each member is responsible to help the group keep our primary purpose in focus.

Unity is one of our greatest strengths in carrying the message. Unity of purpose keeps our focus on carrying the message. As groups, we work together to ensure not only our own personal recovery but the recovery of every NA member. The evidence of many addicts staying clean and seeking our common good is very persuasive. We don't recover alone.

In anonymity, our personal differences are insignificant compared to our primary purpose. When we come together as a group, our first task is to carry the message; all else ought to be set aside. Groups can practice the Fifth Tradition by reminding their members that the recovery message, not individual personalities, is primary in Narcotics Anonymous.

Narcotics Anonymous is a fellowship with meetings around the world. Our primary purpose is a common thread that unites us. Tradition Five defines the focus of Narcotics Anonymous. This focus also helps to ensure our survival as a fellowship. The Fifth Tradition asks us to serve other addicts by carrying the message that recovery is possible in Narcotics Anonymous. This concentrated focus protects the integrity of our fellowship.

TRADITION SIX

*"An NA group ought never endorse, finance,
or lend the NA name to any related facility
or outside enterprise, lest problems of money,
property, or prestige divert us from our
primary purpose."*

While each group has but one primary purpose, there are many ways to fulfill that purpose. Our groups often go to great lengths to carry the message. We carry out our primary purpose as individuals, as groups, and through our service structure. In carrying the message, groups come in contact with other organizations in their areas. Good public relations can help our groups better fulfill their primary purpose, but cooperation with other organizations can also lead to conflict, diverting our groups from carrying the message. Tradition Six tempers our zeal to carry the message, establishing boundaries for our relations with others in the area.

Our fellowship's primary purpose defines us. We are a society of addicts sharing with others the hope of recovery in Narcotics Anonymous. When NA's identity becomes too closely tied to the identity of another organization, the clarity of our primary purpose is muddied, losing some of its power.

The Sixth Tradition warns us of three things that could blur the distinction between Narcotics Anonymous and other enterprises: endorsement, financing, and the lending of our name. An endorsement is a public statement of support for another organization. Financing another organization further endorses its purpose. Lending our name to a related facility or outside enterprise—allowing an addiction treatment facility, for example, to call itself The NA Medical Center—is the ultimate endorsement, permanently tying our primary purpose to theirs in the public eye.

By establishing boundaries, the Sixth Tradition helps our groups avoid some of the problems that commonly arise between organizations. If we endorse an organization that later runs into trouble, our reputation will be damaged along with theirs. If we boost an outside enterprise that some find obnoxious, addicts seeking recovery may be discouraged from coming to our meetings. If we voice support for another organization, the public, the addict who still suffers, even our own members might confuse that organization's purpose with ours. If we fund a related facility or outside enterprise, money that could be used to fulfill our own primary purpose is diverted; if we later withdraw that funding, other problems occur. If we finance or lend our name to one organization instead of another, we can be drawn into a conflict between the two. By helping our groups avoid such problems, Tradition Six allows us to devote all our energy to carrying a clear NA message to addicts seeking recovery.

We must exist in the world. It's not possible to be entirely separate, evading all contact with outside agencies. Not only is it impossible, it's not a good idea. Cooperation with others is healthy for Narcotics Anonymous. Contacts between our groups and the public help others understand NA better. They help increase public goodwill toward NA. They lead doctors, teachers, police, friends, and relatives to recommend NA to addicts who want recovery. They help us carry the message to addicts who can't get to regular meetings. Letting others know who we are and what we offer increases the chance that addicts seeking recovery will hear our message.

NA groups often cultivate good relations with nearby treatment facilities. They make it known that their meetings are always open to addicts from these facilities and make them welcome when they visit. There's a difference, though, between cooperation and endorsement. When a group's primary purpose becomes blurred by its relationship with some other facility or organization, it's time for the group to step back and examine that relationship. For instance, when a group or an area holds a dance, should it offer a reduced entry price to patients from such facilities? Why not just extend such reductions to all newcomers? We should ask these kinds of questions whenever our group's relationship with a related facility or outside enterprise becomes so close that our group appears to be linked with the other organization. By asking ourselves these questions, we help ensure that our cooperation with an outside agency does not inadvertently become an endorsement of that agency.

There are many related facilities and outside enterprises devoted to understanding addiction and aiding recovery. Like NA, each has its particular primary purpose that is reflected in its literature and its message. While that purpose may be similar to ours, it will not be the same as ours because the organization is separate from us. We use NA literature and speakers in our meetings to help us fulfill NA's primary purpose. An NA group that uses another organization's literature or speakers endorses that organization's primary purpose, not ours.

Although a few NA groups meet in their own buildings, most do not. Those who rent meeting space from other organizations need to take special care never to endorse, finance, or lend the NA name to the organizations from which they rent their meeting space. For instance, is the group paying substantially more to meet in a particular facility than it would somewhere else? Does this make it appear that the group endorses the facility in which it meets? Is the group better able to carry the NA message by meeting at that facility, or is the group funding an outside enterprise with its ''rent'' payment? When we devote our energies and funds to carrying the NA message, we free ourselves from distractions or confusion with the primary purpose of other organizations.

It's important to remember that we as NA members and groups are responsible for observing our Twelve

Traditions. The facilities in which we meet do not have this responsibility; neither do other organizations. If it appears that some outside organization or facility is compromising our traditions, we are responsible to discuss their actions with them. While we cannot demand that they change their behavior, a reasonable approach and open discussion will often lead to mutually satisfactory solutions.

A group's meetings provide a forum in which individual members can share their recovery with one another. The message we carry in our meetings can either enhance our efforts to fulfill our primary purpose or distract us from it. Each of us can play a part in carrying out Tradition Six by asking ourselves, "What do I do to clarify NA's relations with other organizations?" Many of us use a variety of resources in our personal programs of recovery and spiritual growth. Not all of them, however, relate directly to NA's primary purpose. Do we imply an endorsement of a related facility or outside enterprise when we share in an NA meeting about the good things we've found elsewhere? Do we distract other members at the meeting from NA's message of recovery or give new members the wrong impression about the Narcotics Anonymous program? No one can answer these questions for us. But by answering these questions for ourselves, we can each help free our group of problems that could divert us from our primary purpose.

Applying spiritual principles

The application of principles is the basis of our freedom. When we adhere to the principles of recovery, we are free to carry the message and interact with others, knowing that we will not compromise our purpose. Some of the principles that help us observe Tradition Six include humility, integrity, faith, harmony, and anonymity.

Humility reminds us of NA's role in society. We have a program that has provided much help to many addicts seeking recovery. We do not, however, have any other purpose in society than to carry the NA message, nor do we pretend that Narcotics Anonymous offers anything more than freedom from active addiction. It may be tempting to think of other good things we might do in the world or for each other if we extended our focus or closely allied ourselves with a wide range of related facilities or outside enterprises. These grandiose dreams serve only to divert us from our primary purpose. Carrying our message to the still-suffering addict is sufficient for us.

Carrying a clear message of recovery in NA reflects integrity. Our message is outlined in our Twelve Steps and Twelve Traditions and further articulated in NA literature. Because our message is also our identity, we take care not to confuse it with the beliefs or literature of other organizations.

We demonstrate faith when we don't trade our endorsement, funds, or name for the cooperation of others. It's true that our friends in society can help us carry our message to addicts who need us. But our faith lies in the effectiveness of our message and the Higher Power that guides our recovery, not in the related facilities and outside enterprises we deal with. If a relationship with another organization compromises our devotion to carrying the recovery message, we need not be afraid to let go of that relationship. Our strength is in the power of the NA program. After all, it works!

The principle of harmony is both assumed and supported by Tradition Six. Our groups seek to cooperate with others in society whenever possible and as much as possible. Our contacts with others are made simple and straightforward when we let them know, right from the start, how far we can go in cooperating with them. By respecting the Sixth Tradition's boundaries in our group's relations with other organizations, we generate harmony in those relations.

Our identity as a fellowship is founded in anonymity and selfless service, carrying the message one addict to another. The relationships we have with outside organizations are not based on the personalities of our leaders; our groups themselves are responsible for their cooperation with other organizations, making those contacts stronger and more effective.

Additionally, anonymity helps us avoid blurring our purpose in our contacts with other organizations. Our relationships with outside agencies exist to help us fulfill our primary purpose, not merely to build our reputation or prestige. When we observe the spirit of anonymity, we seek nothing other than to carry the recovery message to the addict who still suffers.

Within the limits established by Tradition Six, we have tremendous freedom to carry the message of recovery and help other addicts. We have clear boundaries set by our identity as Narcotics Anonymous. When we take care to observe those boundaries, our outside relationships enhance our ability to carry the message to the addict who still suffers rather than diverting us from our primary purpose.

TRADITION SEVEN

"Every NA group ought to be fully self-supporting, declining outside contributions."

The Seventh Tradition adds further clarity to our group's public relations. Tradition Six cautioned us against funding other organizations, lest problems of money, property, or prestige divert us from our primary purpose. Tradition Seven encourages us to decline funding from other organizations for the same reason: to maintain our group's focus on its primary purpose. By paying our own expenses, we remain free to carry our own message.

We encourage every NA group to be fully self-supporting. We also recognize that many meetings don't start that way. Some meetings are started by one or two NA members who want to help carry the message to other addicts. Frequently, such members pay rent and buy literature for these meetings out of their own pockets. Sometimes they're given help by established NA groups or by the nearest area committee. Either way, it may take some time before a new meeting is able to stand on its own feet.

Other meetings—for instance, many in institutions— are started by nonmember professionals who've become acquainted with the Narcotics Anonymous program. Wanting to provide their clients with access to what NA has to offer, these professionals set a time, find a room, buy some literature, give a *Group Booklet* to the addicts who've gathered, and help them start a meeting. After some exposure to the principles underlying the NA program, these recovering addicts begin taking responsibility for their meetings themselves.

How a meeting is begun is not nearly so important as how it grows. Our experience is that, once a meeting is established, it gathers momentum. The meeting begins attracting a group of addicts who attend on a fairly consistent basis. These addicts share their experiences with one another and help each other better understand NA's principles of recovery. At this point, the meeting becomes more than just an event; an NA group has evolved from the meeting, complete with members. With the evolution of an NA group, its members committed to supporting one another, the group as a whole is ready to take full responsibility for its obligations.

Many of us think of the Seventh Tradition as the money tradition. While we have come to associate this tradition of self-support with the funds we contribute, the spirit of the Seventh Tradition goes much farther than that. Whatever a group needs to fulfill its primary purpose should be provided by the group itself.

The question then is, what does a group need? First and foremost, it needs a message to carry—and that, it already has. In the course of its evolution, the group has attracted members who've proven to one another that an addict, any addict, can stop using drugs, lose the desire to use, and find a new way to live. Without that message, the group has no reason to exist; with it, an NA group needs little more.

Beyond that, the needs of the group are simple. Groups need to rent meeting places where their members can gather and where newcomers can find them. Most groups find it important to buy NA literature which they make available at their meetings. The expenses associated with these things may be substantial, yet most groups can meet such expenses by passing the hat.

After paying their basic expenses, most groups contribute to the NA boards and committees that serve them. Phonelines, meeting lists, NA literature, H&I panels, and public information presentations all benefit the group. That's why service contributions are just as surely a part of a group's self-support obligation as the rent for its meeting room. Like the groups, NA service boards and committees decline contributions from sources outside the fellowship. Unlike the groups, however, our service boards and committees are not themselves fully self-supporting. They have been created to help the groups fulfill their primary purpose more effectively, and they depend on group contributions for the money they need to do their work.

To fulfill its purpose, the group also needs some things that don't cost a penny. A group needs someone to open its meeting room, set up the chairs, and prepare the literature table. In some groups, a member offers to prepare refreshments, helping establish a hospitable environment for the newcomer. Most importantly, a group needs the consistent commitment of its members to show up and take part in its meetings. Upon that commitment rests the group's stability; without it, no group can survive long. From the commitment of its members, the group also draws its ability to carry our recovery message. Group service and active group membership are two vital contributions to group self-support, contributions that don't cost any money at all.

As simple as a group's needs are, a group's decision to become fully self-supporting does not usually require the commitment of extensive amounts of its members' money, time, or other resources. If a group is having problems sustaining itself, it may want to ask itself some questions: What is our primary purpose, and how do we fulfill it? What does our group need to fulfill its primary purpose? Have we confused our wants with our needs? When a group's sense of its needs have become unreasonable, the simplicity of the Fifth Tradition can help deflate those needs to their proper size.

But what if a group is still unable to pay its own way even after examining its understanding of the Fifth Tradition? Tradition Seven tells our groups that they should not seek outside contributions—but why not? What considerations keep us from seeking money outside the NA Fellowship?

First, the group will want to consider its identity as a part of the Fellowship of Narcotics Anonymous.

Recovery in NA is very different in a number of ways from our using. When we were using, many of us took whatever we could from whomever we could as often as we could. Our group's decision to become fully self-supporting, declining outside contributions, reflects the new way our members are living in recovery. Rather than taking what we want or need from others, we are paying our own way.

The group will also want to examine its identity as a group. When we were using, most of us looked out for ourselves and ourselves alone, not giving any thought for one another's welfare. An NA recovery group, on the other hand, is founded on its members' commitment to one another. Many of us have tried to find a way of making it on our own, but without success. We've found we need one another to survive and to grow. The NA group is both the expression and the fulfillment of that need we have for one another's support. An NA group reinforces the solidarity of its members and the foundation of their continued recovery by declining outside contributions.

"Alright," we say, "our group has made a commitment to become fully self-supporting. But what if the money we collect from passing the hat still isn't sufficient to meet our needs? What if we sold some T-shirts or jewelry to raise some cash or held a dinner and asked for a donation at the door? Perhaps the energy our members put into such activities could be turned into the money we need to pay our bills."

On the face of it, there doesn't seem to be any contradiction between the Seventh Tradition and these kinds of money-raising activities. Before engaging in such activities, however, the group might want to ask itself some questions. First, of course, is the question of need. For what purpose does the group seek these funds? We might also ask ourselves whether such activities, intended to raise money to help our group carry the message, might end up diverting us from carrying the message. Money-raising activities usually take a good bit of time to manage, time that might be better spent in fulfilling our primary purpose more directly. If fundraising activities are successful, bringing in more money than the group needs to meet its obligations, controversy over control of that money may well arise, distracting the group from its primary purpose. A group may also want to consider whether the atmosphere created by selling goods and services at its meetings might detract from the free, open atmosphere so conducive to recovery.

By and large, our groups have found that the simplest, straightest path to full self-support is through the voluntary contributions of their own members. For this reason, we discourage groups from engaging in fundraising activities. If a group is unable to provide for its own needs from the contributions of its members, perhaps group members will want to consider increasing their contributions.

In the same breath as we speak of this, however, we need also recall our fellowship's Third Tradition, which affirms that the only requirement for membership is a desire to stop using. Our membership, whether we are speaking of membership in NA as a whole or group membership, does not depend on the amount of money we give; indeed, we aren't required to give any money at all in order to consider ourselves NA members.

If our group has carefully examined its expenses, trimmed them to match only what it needs to fulfill its primary purpose, and still doesn't bring in enough money to pay its own way, the group's members will be left with some questions only they can answer for themselves, individually: What do I get from the group? Does my personal recovery depend on its survival? Am I able to give more than I've already given and still meet my own financial responsibilities?

At the same time as we consider our levels of personal contributions to the group, we should remember that Tradition Seven speaks of the *group* as being self-supporting, not of one or two well-off group members paying all the group's expenses or doing all its work. Later, in the chapters on Traditions Nine and Twelve, we will look at rotating leadership as a way to keep a group, service board, or committee from becoming a mere extension of one or two members' personalities. In the same way, the Seventh Tradition encourages the NA group as a whole to support itself, avoiding financial dependence on one member or another. We each do well in giving our part toward the group's self-support obligations without making the group overly dependent on our individual contributions.

In the end, our individual decisions and group commitments are entirely up to us because we are the ones who have to live with them. However, certain lines from our White Booklet, written in reference to the Twelve Steps, seem to apply equally to the observance of the Seventh Tradition—indeed, to all the traditions: "If you want what we have to offer, and are willing to make the effort to get it . . . these are the principles that made our recovery possible." If we want what the group has to offer us individually, and if our group wants to reap the benefits associated with self-support, we will practice the principles that make those things possible.

Applying spiritual principles

Our Twelve Traditions describe those specific things that have been found to help our groups remain strong, lively, and free. Underlying the specifics of our traditions, however, are dozens of spiritual principles, any one of which could be applied to almost any of the Twelve Traditions. This broad field of principle is the ground upon which the traditions have grown. The more we cultivate this ground, the stronger our understanding and application of each of the traditions themselves will be. Some of the principles which will strengthen our appreciation of the Seventh Tradition are gratitude, responsibility, faith, integrity, anonymity, and freedom.

The gratitude we speak of in regard to Tradition Seven is like the collective sense of direction the Second Tradition talks about; it is the gratitude of the NA group as a group. When NA members gather to share their recovery, they generate a sense of gratitude among themselves. They are grateful the group exists and want it to continue to be there for them and for the members yet to come. The gratitude of the group speaks, in part, through the group's collective commitment to support itself.

The group's decision to become fully self-supporting, declining outside contributions, reflects the group's sense of responsibility for itself. In recovery, we discard the illusion that the rest of the world is responsible to take care of us; rather, we take due pride in caring for ourselves. Individually, we demonstrate our newfound maturity by accepting the weight of our own burdens; collectively, we demonstrate our maturity by accepting responsibility for our group, neither seeking nor accepting outside contributions.

The burden of responsibility, however, may seem unbearable without an appreciation for the simplicity of the group's needs. The commitment to become self-supporting is not a commitment to raise vast sums of money to fulfill sweeping programs. Rather, the group determines it will muster the few basic resources it needs to fulfill its simple primary purpose: to carry the message to the still-suffering addict. The ideal of simplicity, when applied to Tradition Seven, helps our groups avoid the heated conflicts that often arise over the control of great resources. Problems of money, property, and prestige need not divert our groups from their primary purpose when the simplicity of that purpose and of our needs is kept squarely in focus.

In understanding the principles underlying the Seventh Tradition, practical simplicity walks hand in hand with our faith in a Higher Power. So long as we take our direction from that Power, our needs are met. Likewise, the decision to decline outside contributions, meeting the group's needs from the group's own resources, is based firmly in faith. So long as our group remains devoted to fulfilling its primary purpose, its needs are met.

As members of an NA group, we have made a commitment to support one another in our recovery. Our group's commitment to become fully self-supporting reflects the group's integrity, its faithfulness to its fundamental identity. We support each other in recovery and, together, we fulfill our collective responsibilities as members of a self-supporting group.

The anonymity we exercise in accepting our group responsibilities reflects our integrity. The anonymity of the Seventh Tradition means more than just contributing anonymously, without thought of recognition, though of course it does involve that. Anonymity in the context of Tradition Seven also means that all the contributions of a group's members are important. Money put in the basket, time put into setting up the meeting room, energy put into making newcomers welcome—all are part of the responsibility of the group, and all are equally important contributions to the self-supporting NA group.

Our anonymity, our integrity, our faith, our sense of simplicity, our acceptance of responsibility, our gratitude—together, all these things spell freedom. By encouraging our group to pay its own way, the Seventh Tradition gives our group the freedom to share its recovery as it sees fit, not obligated to outside contributors. Further, it gives our group the freedom that comes from inner strength, the strength that develops through applying spiritual principles. By making the decision to become fully self-supporting, our NA group assures that it will always have the resources it needs to survive and continue fulfilling its primary purpose.

TRADITION EIGHT

"Narcotics Anonymous should remain forever nonprofessional, but our service centers may employ special workers."

Narcotics Anonymous offers a distinctly nonprofessional approach to the disease of addiction. We have no hospitals, no treatment centers, no outpatient clinics, none of the facilities associated with a professional enterprise. We do not diagnose anyone's condition or track the progress of our patients—in fact, we have no patients, only members. Our groups do not provide professional therapeutic, medical, legal, or psychiatric services. We are simply a fellowship of recovering addicts who meet regularly to help each other stay clean.

In discussing the Sixth Tradition, we considered the sufficiency of our message. Narcotics Anonymous groups need not rely on outside enterprises in order to effectively offer recovery from addiction. In the same way, Tradition Eight reminds us that our members need no professional credentials to be effective in carrying the NA message. The heart of the NA way of recovery from addiction is one addict helping another. We have no certified NA counselors; our varied experiences in recovery from drug addiction are all the credentials we need. The first-hand exposure each of us has in recovery from addiction is more than sufficient to qualify us to carry the message to other addicts. Our members are not paid a salary for their Twelfth Step work, nor do our groups charge any dues or fees for carrying the NA message. This is what we mean when we say that Narcotics Anonymous should remain forever non-professional.

This is not to say that a member of Narcotics Anonymous should never take a job as a professional therapist of one sort or another. It is only to say that, at an NA meeting, a member's vocation is irrelevant. The therapeutic value in the message we share with one another lies in our personal experience in recovery, not in our credentials, our training, or our professional status.

We don't sell recovery; we share it freely with others in a spirit of love and gratitude. However, Narcotics Anonymous groups, service boards, and committees may require professional help in fulfilling their responsibilities. Tradition Eight makes a distinction between "selling our recovery" and paying people to help us do our service work. If one of our committees requires professional assistance in a service task, it's alright, for example, to contract the help of a lawyer or an accountant. If we need to employ someone to help us on a regular basis, a "special worker," we may give them a paycheck in return for the services they provide us. Special workers who are also NA members are not selling their recovery. They are simply providing professional service support we would otherwise have to hire nonaddicts to provide.

Applying spiritual principles

Tradition Eight is one of the simplest, most straightforward of the Twelve Traditions. Likewise, the principles underlying the Eighth Tradition are eminently practical ones: humility, prudence, anonymity, and integrity.

An NA group exercises humility when it does not pretend to be anything more or less than it is. We do not claim to be professionals or experts in anything. We are not physicians, psychiatrists, or therapists; we are recovering addicts. All we offer is our collective practical experience in getting clean and learning to live clean. The value of our program comes from the identification and trust that exist between one addict and another.

We further exercise humility when we recognize that sometimes we need professionals to help us fulfill our services. We place great emphasis on the therapeutic value of one addict helping another, sometimes to the extent that we are reluctant to hire professional assistance when we need it. But some NA services require too much time or expertise for our members to fulfill on a strictly volunteer basis. We mustn't allow our pride to prevent our fellowship from hiring the help it needs to support its services.

Neither should we hire special workers for jobs we can do ourselves. We must exercise prudence in employing professional assistance for our services. Most NA service responsibilities do not require special expertise or large, consistent commitments of time.

Our members are perfectly capable of fulfilling such responsibilities on a volunteer basis. By exercising prudence, we can distinguish between those tasks requiring the support of special workers and those we can fulfill voluntarily.

The Eighth Tradition reminds our groups of the value of anonymity. Professionals are people with certain specialized skills, often recognized by the credentials given them by a certifying panel. An NA group has no such recognized experts. All group members are experts in their own recovery, fully qualified to share that recovery with another addict.

Finally, Tradition Eight supports the integrity of the NA group by helping it preserve what is most important about its fundamental identity. What is Narcotics Anonymous, after all, but a fellowship of addicts freely sharing with one another the simple message of their own experience? The Eighth Tradition is a firm, permanent commitment on the part of each NA group to steadfastly maintain the feature of our program that is, indeed, of foremost value. By agreeing that Narcotics Anonymous should remain forever nonprofessional, we reaffirm our belief that the therapeutic value of one addict helping another is without parallel! This is the heart of our program; so long as that heart beats strongly, our fellowship and our recovery shall remain vital.

TRADITION NINE

*"NA, as such, ought never be organized, but
we may create service boards or committees
directly responsible to those they serve."*

In our White Booklet, we read that "NA is a nonprofit
fellowship or society of men and women for whom
drugs had become a major problem. We are
recovering addicts who meet regularly to help each
other stay clean." This is NA, as such—a simple
fellowship using a nonprofessional, addict-to-addict
approach to the disease of addiction. We are a
fellowship, not a lobbying organization or a medical
service or a chain of treatment facilities. We are
nonprofessional. We have no rules, no fees, no
governing bodies, and only one membership
requirement: a desire to stop using. Our primary
purpose is, quite simply, to carry the message. These
are some of the traditional standards by which our
groups may guide themselves, and our ultimate
guiding authority is a Higher Power as it finds
expression in the conscience of our members. That's
NA, as such, as we understand it. Our groups work
as well as they do because they keep it simple, lest
anything get in the way of carrying our message as
simply and directly as possible, one addict to another.

Yet for all its emphasis on keeping things simple,
Tradition Nine is not an excuse for *dis*-organized
service work; instead, it recognizes that our fellowship

does require a certain degree of organization to fulfill its primary purpose. Rather than recommend that NA groups themselves become organized, the Ninth Tradition suggests that groups organize separate boards and committees to serve their needs. Just as we are nonprofessional but may hire professionals to help us, so we are not organized but may organize boards or committees to serve us. This arrangement ensures that NA, as such, maintains its uncluttered, direct approach to recovery while assuring our ability to fulfill service tasks requiring a certain amount of organization.

Okay, so we may create service boards or committees. Now we must ask ourselves, why would we want to create such things? What are the needs these boards and committees would fulfill? To answer this question, let's look at how an NA group evolves, as we did when considering the Seventh Tradition.

In the beginning, an area's first NA group only needs to gather its members together so they can help one another stay clean and carry their message to other addicts. As the group grows, it begins taking care of a variety of business related to its meetings, trying to ensure that the message is carried as effectively as possible. To maintain the focus of its recovery meetings, the group usually conducts its business meeting separately, keeping NA, as such, as simple as possible.

As the group grows even larger, it often sprouts new groups. To maintain some of the unity and camaraderie that existed when there was only one group in the area, these groups elect representatives who meet periodically. These representatives share information with one another about how their individual groups are doing and help one another find solutions to problems one group or another may be having. From time to time, they may even organize a joint recovery meeting or social activity, gathering the entire NA community together.

Sooner or later, the groups realize the potential they have in this committee of representatives. Through this committee, the groups can combine their guidance and resources so that each of them can function more effectively and all, together, can carry the message farther. The groups may ask their committee to buy bulk supplies of literature, making it easier for each group to procure NA books and pamphlets. The groups might ask their committee to compile a directory for distribution at meetings throughout the area, making it easier for addicts to find out where NA meetings are being held. The groups may ask that public information, hospitals and institutions, and phoneline programs be set up, letting still-suffering addicts who might not hear of NA by word of mouth know of the fellowship's existence and increasing general awareness of Narcotics Anonymous. The point is, the development of these services is based squarely on the groups' needs. We create these boards and committees to serve us in fulfilling those needs.

First, the groups define their needs; then, they create the boards and committees which will serve them. Once created, how do we assure that our service boards and committees will remain directly responsible to those they serve? We do this, first and foremost, through consistent communication. Through their representatives, groups communicate with the boards and committees serving them. The groups provide regular information about their condition and their activities. They communicate their concerns, their needs, their ideas, and their wishes. This information helps our boards and committees better understand and serve the needs of the groups.

Communication is a two-way street. Groups share information and guidance with the boards and committees serving them. Then these boards and committees report back to the groups to which they are responsible, describing their operations, discussions, and plans. Responsible service boards and committees consult the groups in matters directly affecting them and seek direction from the groups in matters not already covered by existing policy. By maintaining regular two-way communication between NA groups and the boards and committees serving them, we create an atmosphere of responsibility that serves our fellowship and its primary purpose well.

Applying spiritual principles

Because the Ninth Tradition empowers the groups to establish a service structure—not a simple thing—

many of us think of Tradition Nine as being very complex. In reality, the spiritual principles underlying this tradition are very simple. The Ninth Tradition focuses, first, not on the relationship between groups and service committees but on NA, as such. We are a fellowship of recovering addicts who help one another stay clean, nothing more.

Whenever possible, organized service work should be kept distinct from the groups so that they can remain free to simply and directly fulfill our primary purpose, addict to addict. The boards and committees we do organize, we organize on the basis of need only, using the simplest guidelines possible. We organize them solely to serve us, not to establish a complex governing bureaucracy. The Ninth Tradition is far from complicated; in fact, it speaks throughout of simplicity.

In the same way, Tradition Nine speaks of anonymity. When the Ninth Tradition exhorts NA, as such, never to become organized, it is telling us that we ought not create a governing hierarchy, a top-down bureaucracy dictating to our groups and members. As we noted in the Second Tradition, our leaders are not governors but servants taking their directions from the collective conscience of those they serve. Our primary purpose, not the personalities of our trusted servants, is what defines NA, as such. To reinforce the anonymity of Tradition Nine, our groups, service boards, and committees practice various systems of rotating leadership so that no one personality ever dominates.

Another principle implicit in the Ninth Tradition is the principle of humility. Each group on its own is somewhat limited in its ability to fulfill its primary purpose; it has only so many members, so much time, and so many dollars to use in carrying the message by itself. However, when a number of groups combine their resources by joining together to form a service board or committee, they enhance their ability to fulfill their primary purpose. Together, they become able to do what they could not do alone.

The principle of humility also applies to the boards and committees spoken of in our Ninth Tradition. These boards and committees are established to serve only, not to govern. They are directly responsible to the groups and are always subject to the explicit direction of the groups. Although our service boards and committees may do much to help our groups fulfill their primary purpose, it is in the groups where NA, as such, comes to focus, not in the boards and committees that serve them.

Prudence is one of the guiding principles behind the Ninth Tradition relationship between the groups and the boards or committees that serve them. Groups are responsible to consider their needs carefully, planning prudently before they create boards and committees. There is nothing that will complicate the simplicity of NA, as such, more than a needlessly elaborate array of committees, boards, and subcommittees.

The groups' responsibility does not end with the establishment of a board or committee to fulfill their service needs; in fact, that is only the beginning. As long as the committee remains active, the groups should maintain familiarity with its affairs. The groups should also provide continuing guidance to the committee. Our boards and committees cannot be held accountable to the groups they serve unless the groups play a responsible role in their service relationships.

Finally, the Ninth Tradition speaks of fidelity. Narcotics Anonymous groups join together, combining their resources to create service boards and committees that will help them better fulfill their primary purpose. Those boards and committees are not called to govern Narcotics Anonymous; they are called, rather, to faithfully execute the trust given them by the groups they serve. With a minimum of organization, our service boards and committees perform tasks on behalf of the groups, helping our groups remain free to do what they do best, simply and directly. Our fidelity to the Ninth Tradition assures that the simple, spontaneous atmosphere of recovery shared one addict to another in the NA group is never organized, legislated, or regulated out of existence.

TRADITION TEN

*"Narcotics Anonymous has no opinion on
outside issues; hence, the NA name ought
never be drawn into public controversy."*

Narcotics Anonymous is a society of recovering
addicts who help one another stay clean by applying
certain simple spiritual principles. Our primary
purpose, as groups and as a fellowship, is to offer that
same help to any addict seeking recovery. Aside from
that, NA has no opinions whatsoever. By refusing to
take sides on other issues, we avoid becoming
embroiled in public controversies that could distract
us from our primary purpose. This is the message of
our Tenth Tradition.

To most of us, it probably seems obvious that
Narcotics Anonymous, as a fellowship, has no opinion
on the pressing world issues of our day. Most of these
issues have little to do with either addiction or
recovery. But there are a great number of addiction-
related issues that others might expect a worldwide
society of recovering drug addicts to take positions
on. "What is NA's opinion," we are sometimes asked,
"on the addiction treatment industry, other twelve-
step fellowships, the legalization of drugs, addiction-
related illnesses, and all the rest?" Our answer,
according to Tradition Ten, is that our groups and our
fellowship take no position, pro or con, on any issues
except the NA program itself. We maintain neutrality

on such issues so that we can maintain our focus on what we do best: sharing recovery from one addict to another.

However, even in explaining our own program in public, we may find ourselves treading on controversial ground. NA's views on total abstinence, on the possibility of recovering in society without long-term institutionalization, on the disease concept of addiction, even our broad views on spirituality are not met with universal acceptance. Others who deal with addiction and recovery may view these matters very differently than we do. We cannot deny those aspects of our program that others take exception to. We can, however, take care to explain our program in such a way as not to invite controversy deliberately. "We do not suggest that everyone adopt our views, nor do we oppose those with different views," we can explain. "We simply want you to know what the Narcotics Anonymous program is like." So long as we focus, as groups and as a fellowship, on our recovery experience rather than our opinions of why or how NA works, we will stay as far as possible from public controversy.

Tradition Ten restricts NA, as a fellowship, from stating opinions on outside issues. However, it places no such restriction on the individual member. In Narcotics Anonymous, we believe strongly in personal freedom. Addicts who have a desire to stop using can become members of NA simply by saying so. We have no dues or fees, no pledges to sign, no promises to make to anyone, ever. Though a spiritual program, we encourage our members to develop their own understanding of a Higher Power. Even our leaders are only trusted servants, with no power to tell individual members what to do, think, or say. NA members are encouraged to think for themselves, to develop their own opinions, and to express those opinions as they see fit.

The only caution Tradition Ten offers individual NA members is that, when speaking publicly, we think through what we're going to say before we say it. In certain situations, anything an NA member says will be taken as NA's opinion, even when the situation itself has nothing to do with Narcotics Anonymous and the member clearly states that the views expressed are strictly personal. It's not our fault if others misinterpret what we say as individuals; this does not, however, make the complications arising from such misinterpretations any less serious for NA. We may be able to avoid such complications before they arise simply by thinking carefully before we speak in public.

But what about speaking in a recovery gathering? Does the Tenth Tradition tell us that, as individual recovering addicts, we must not talk in NA meetings about the challenges we face? No, it does not. While a particular problem may be an outside issue, its effect on our recovery is not; everything affecting a recovering addict's life is material for sharing. If a problem we are having impacts our ability to stay clean and grow spiritually, it's not an outside issue.

Many things can put us off balance and challenge our recovery. We often discuss such challenges with one another at our meetings, seeking to ease our personal burdens by sharing them with our fellow NA members. We ask others to share how they have applied the principles of the program in similar circumstances, recovering their balance and strengthening their recovery. We need no one's permission to talk about such things in our meetings.

But, for all that, we all know that controversial personal opinions can distract our meetings from their primary purpose. If everything is recovery material, yet we want to help our meetings retain their focus on recovery, how do we decide what to share? We can ask ourselves some questions: Am I sharing from my experience, or am I expounding an opinion? As an individual, am I dwelling in the problem or seeking the solution? Do I share to draw the group together or to force the group into separate camps? Do I make it clear that what I say, I say for myself, *not* for Narcotics Anonymous? So long as we keep our common welfare and our primary purpose in focus, we will avoid the kind of controversy that distracts us from recovery.

Applying spiritual principles

Foremost among the principles our groups and our fellowship apply in practicing Tradition Ten is the principle of unity. For all the diversity of individual opinion among our members, Narcotics Anonymous itself is united in having no opinion on any issues apart from its own program. As a fellowship, we agree to take positions only on those ideas that have drawn us together, our principles of recovery, not on the many personal opinions that might divide us.

The Tenth Tradition is an exercise in responsibility. As groups and as a fellowship, we are responsible to carry our message to the still-suffering addict. We are responsible to provide an atmosphere in which recovering addicts can share freely with one another. To do these things effectively, we must stay as free of the distractions of public controversy as possible. We may not be able to avoid all public controversy, because various features of the Narcotics Anonymous program itself—such as our views on total abstinence—may arouse a certain amount of contention in some public quarters. However, we absolutely can avoid any controversies which might arise from groups or the fellowship taking positions on issues entirely outside the scope of our program.

Individual NA members responsibly exercise the Tenth Tradition by personally guarding NA's neutrality whenever and wherever they speak. Publicly, we differentiate between our personal opinions and those of NA, avoiding the expression of any personal opinions at all in circumstances where the difference might not be recognized. In meetings, NA members make it clear that what we share is our own experience, not the position of Narcotics Anonymous, providing as little opportunity as possible for misinterpretation. The way we speak as NA members often affects how others view NA; therefore, as responsible members, we speak carefully, guarding the neutrality that is so important to the welfare of us all.

To fulfill Tradition Ten, our groups, service boards, and committees must exercise prudence in their public contacts. Elements of our fellowship are constantly in touch with others in society. Groups maintain contacts with their meeting facilities and those in their neighborhoods; H&I subcommittees, with facility administrators; public information workers, with health professionals, charitable organizations, government agencies, and the media. In all our contacts with society, we must take care not to express any opinions on issues outside the scope of our program. Such prudence will protect our credibility in the public eye on the only issue that truly concerns Narcotics Anonymous: our program of recovery from addiction.

By practicing the Tenth Tradition, we demonstrate our belief in the value of anonymity. All of us have our opinions. But when we speak as groups and as a fellowship, we do not take positions on the opinions of individuals. What we have to share with the public is our fellowship's message, not our personal opinions.

Tradition Ten is supremely practical. The only issue upon which our fellowship is willing to publicly stake its reputation is the NA program itself. Underlying the practicality of the Tenth Tradition, however, can be found a fundamental spiritual principle, that of humility. Narcotics Anonymous does not claim to have the answer to every trouble in the world. We do not even claim that we necessarily have the only answer to addiction. When we share in public, as groups or as a fellowship, we share only our message. We talk about what we do, neither supporting nor opposing what anyone else does. We are what we are, and that's all that we are: a society of recovering drug addicts sharing their recovery with one another and offering the same to the addict who still suffers. We speak simply about our program, knowing that our effectiveness will attract more goodwill than any amount of promotion. Our program has worked for us and is available for others interested in recovery. If we can be of service, we stand ready to help.

TRADITION ELEVEN

*"Our public relations policy is based on
attraction rather than promotion; we need
always maintain personal anonymity at the
level of press, radio, and films."*

The Eleventh Tradition is the cornerstone of NA's
public relations policy. But Tradition Eleven is only
one of six traditions that address various aspects of
our relations with the public. The Third and Fifth
Traditions talk about the primary purpose and ultimate
target of our public relations efforts. Traditions Six and
Seven describe the nature of our relations with other
organizations, and the Tenth Tradition details our
policy concerning public pronouncements on issues
outside the scope of our recovery program. Clearly,
our traditions are just as concerned with our public
relations as they are with our internal relations.

Most NA groups have some sort of contact with the
public in their everyday affairs. But the public relations
spoken of in the Eleventh Tradition are more
deliberate than our group's routine encounters with
those outside the fellowship. The existence of a public
relations "policy" implies the importance of a public
relations "program" in carrying out our fellowship's
primary purpose. Public information work, done
properly, *is not* promotion; rather, it seeks to make NA
attractive to those who might need us. As NA

groups, service boards, and committees, we deliberately and energetically cultivate good public relations, not as an incidental result of our normal activity but as a way to better carry our message to addicts. Narcotics Anonymous is not a secret society; Tradition Eleven speaks to personal anonymity, not fellowship anonymity. The better known we are by the public, the more likely it is that addicts seeking recovery—or their friends, relatives, or co-workers— will think of us and know where to find us when they decide to seek help. One way to take part in NA's public relations program is to become involved in the local public information subcommittee.

The Eleventh Tradition tells us that, when we engage in public relations activity, we are to speak simply and directly of what Narcotics Anonymous is and what we do. We are not to make exaggerated claims about NA. Our public relations efforts should be as inviting and nonpromotional as our program itself, saying to addicts and society at large, "If you want what we have to offer, this is what we are and how we work. If we can be of service, please let us know."

Some organizations use celebrity members as public spokespersons, hoping to enhance the organization's credibility by tying it to the celebrity's status. This may be fine for other organizations. But Tradition Eleven tells us in no uncertain terms that, in NA's public relations efforts, we must never do this—not with celebrity members, not with any member. If our fellowship used a celebrity member in a public announcement about NA and the celebrity later relapsed or otherwise suffered a loss of prestige, what good would that do our fellowship's credibility? The same could apply to any individual member put in the public spotlight on NA's behalf. The credibility of NA's message can be greatly affected by NA's messengers. In the public eye—including press, radio, films, and all other media—we need always maintain personal anonymity.

The same applies to other kinds of public information work. Public anonymity helps keep the focus of our public relations on the NA message, not the PI workers involved. We never do PI work alone because a team—even a pair—better displays NA as a fellowship to the public, while individuals tend to draw attention to themselves. Teams also tend to keep the personalities of their members in check, the better to ensure that NA and not the individual addict is what we present to the public. The truism that "an addict alone is in bad company" applies to our public relations efforts just as well as to our personal recovery.

In most circumstances, though, personal anonymity is a purely personal decision. However closely we may have guarded the secret of our addiction, most of those close to us probably knew we were in trouble when we were using. Today it may be helpful to tell them about our recovery and our membership in Narcotics Anonymous.

Other circumstances may also warrant the disclosure of our NA membership. When a friend tells us about the struggles another person is having with addiction, we may want to let that friend know about Narcotics Anonymous and what it has done for us. When a co-worker has a drug problem, we may want to share our experience with that person. None of us will want to indiscriminately trumpet all the gory details of our addiction to everyone in town, nor will we disclose our NA membership to everyone we meet. When we think we may be helpful to someone, however, it may be appropriate to share a bit of our story and the recovery we've found in Narcotics Anonymous.

All our members play a part in our public relations, whether or not they're involved in public information work. When individual addicts demonstrate recovery at work in their lives, they become our strongest attraction, a living testament of NA's effectiveness. Seeing us now, those who know what we once were like will spread the word to those they meet that NA works. The further that message is carried, the more likely it is that addicts seeking recovery will be attracted to the warm, loving support of our fellowship.

By the same token, we must remember that, wherever we go, we always represent NA to some degree. If we are seen acting poorly while we prominently display an NA logo on our T-shirt, we carry a distinctly unattractive message about our fellowship to the public. What we say and what we do reflects on our NA recovery and the NA Fellowship. As responsible NA members, we want that reflection to be a source of attraction rather than a source of embarrassment.

Applying spiritual principles

Tradition Eleven is an expression of our faith in the effectiveness of our program. As a fellowship, our primary purpose is to carry the recovery message to the still-suffering addict. To fulfill that primary purpose, we do not need a promotional public relations policy. To gain public goodwill and attract addicts to our meetings, all we need to do is clearly and simply describe the Narcotics Anonymous program. We need neither fanfare, overblown claims, nor celebrity endorsements to build our public relations. We have faith that the effectiveness of our fellowship, once made known, will speak for itself.

The principle of service, critical to the application of our Eleventh Tradition, is not a passive principle. To be of maximum service to the still-suffering addict, we must energetically seek to carry our message throughout our cities, towns, and villages. Our public relations policy is based on attraction, to be sure, not promotion. But to attract the still-suffering addict to our program, we must take vigorous steps to make our program widely known. The better and broader our public relations, the better we will be able to serve.

Earlier in this chapter, we spoke of the more practical aspects of public anonymity. But, as we will see in the next chapter, anonymity is far more than just a practical consideration to be taken into account in carrying out our public relations program. Each of us has our own life, our own words, and our own story, all adding dimension and color to the message of our fellowship. But the message we carry to society is not the message of how great we are as individuals. The primary purpose of our public relations efforts is to tell the story of Narcotics Anonymous and what our program offers to the still-suffering addict. Our practice of public anonymity is built on the spiritual foundation of all our traditions, ever reminding us to place principles before personalities.

TRADITION TWELVE

"Anonymity is the spiritual foundation of all
our traditions, ever reminding us to place
principles before personalities."

In personal recovery, we seek to replace self-will with
the guidance of a Higher Power in our personal affairs.
In the same way, the traditions describe a fellowship
that takes its collective guidance from spiritual
principles rather than individual personalities. That
kind of selflessness is what the Twelfth Tradition means
by the word "anonymity," and it is the spiritual foundation upon which Narcotics Anonymous is built.
Tradition Twelve is all the traditions rolled up in one,
summarizing and reinforcing the message of the
previous eleven.

Anonymity is essential in preserving the stability of
our fellowship, making personal recovery possible.
Recovery is a delicate thing. It grows best in a stable,
supportive environment. Each of us and each of our
groups plays a part in maintaining that stability. Our
unity is so precious that, given a choice between
fulfilling our own wishes and preserving our
fellowship's common welfare, we put the best interests
of NA first. We do this not only out of enlightened
self-interest but out of our sense of responsibility to
our fellow addicts. The principle of NA unity comes
before the fulfillment of our personal wishes.

Anonymity is the primary principle underlying our tradition of membership. While we all have our personal differences, NA's only membership requirement is what we have in common: a desire to stop using. This simple principle draws the diverse personalities of those who suffer from our disease together in a common fellowship of recovery.

The principle of anonymity lies at the core of our fellowship's understanding of group conscience. The ideas of each individual group member have their importance, but the group takes its guidance from the collective conscience of all its members. Before the group makes a decision, its members consult their Higher Power, seeking spiritual guidance on the matter at hand. Their individual voices humbly join in developing a collective sense of God's will for the group, and a strong common voice arises out of that mix to guide us all. We call this group conscience. The same principle applies to NA's concept of leadership. Though individual members serve as NA leaders, these leaders act only as our servants, carrying out their duties in accordance with the group conscience. The principles of selfless service and collective guidance come before the personalities of our trusted servants.

Just as the principle of anonymity guides the evolution of a group's collective conscience, so it also applies to group autonomy. Each NA group is, of course, entirely free to fulfill its primary purpose as it sees fit, developing its own way of doing things and its own group personality. Our fellowship places only one restriction on this near-total liberty: The group may not exercise its personality at the expense of neighboring groups or NA as a whole. The welfare of each NA group depends, to an extent, on the welfare of all NA groups. Our groups do not seek ascendancy over one another; rather, they join and cooperate to work for the greater good of the fellowship as a whole. The principle of anonymity draws our autonomous groups together for the common welfare of them all.

The principle of anonymity shapes our primary purpose. Although individual ambition and personal purpose may provide motivation for our development as human beings, our fellowship is guided by its collective purpose: to carry our message to the still-suffering addict. When we enter Narcotics Anonymous, we leave our personal agenda at the door. We seek to help others rather than only ourselves. This selfless principle, not personal ambition, defines the primary purpose of our groups.

Anonymity guides our fellowship's interactions in society. We are not a secret organization; we are happy to see our name becoming better known throughout the world with each passing year. However, we do not trade that name for the endorsement of organizations that might possibly help us further our primary purpose. Nor do we attempt to gain public influence by asserting the prestige of our fellowship's name. If we are fulfilling our primary purpose, society will see our usefulness. We will have no need to trade our endorsement for the support of others. The good spoken of us by our fellowship's friends will be sufficient recommendation.

Anonymity is one of the guiding principles behind the way our groups practice the Seventh Tradition. We believe in the value of selfless generosity for its own sake. For this reason, we choose to receive support from our members anonymously. We also encourage each group as a whole to become fully self-supporting, not dependent on only one or two individual members. The principle of selfless giving, without expectation of personal distinction or reward, goes hand-in-hand with the principle of collective responsibility. Together, they assure both the spiritual solidarity and the financial stability of our groups.

This same principle of selfless anonymity is the spiritual foundation of our Eighth Tradition. In Narcotics Anonymous, we have no professional Twelfth Steppers. Rather, we use the simple language of empathy to freely share with one another the spiritual experience we call recovery. A spiritual experience cannot be bought or sold; it can only be given away. The more we freely share that experience, the more we strengthen the empathy that joins us together. This tradition reminds us to place the principle of anonymous, selfless giving before whatever personal desires we may have for recognition or reward.

In Narcotics Anonymous, we apply the principle of anonymity in the way we structure our service organization. Our fellowship has no authoritarian hierarchy. We create boards and committees solely to serve us, not to govern. The various elements of our service structure are guided by the primary purpose and collective conscience of our fellowship and are held directly accountable for the service they do on our behalf. Those who serve on our various boards and committees are expected to do so not to seek power, property, or prestige for themselves, but to selflessly serve the fellowship that has made their recovery possible.

Almost all our groups, service boards, and committees rotate different members through their service positions, rarely asking one individual to serve in a particular position of responsibility more than one or two terms in a row. The practice of rotation emphasizes our fellowship's belief in the value of anonymity in service. NA service is not primarily a personal endeavor; rather, it is the collective responsibility of our fellowship as a whole. This doesn't mean that we do not appreciate the care, experience, and insight that individuals may offer in carrying out their service duties. However, we place the principle of anonymity in service before the personalities of our individual trusted servants. Collective responsibility, not personal authority, is the guiding force behind NA services.

The principle of anonymity gives form to our fellowship's public voice. Each of our many members has personal opinions on a wide range of subjects.

The public message our fellowship carries, however, is the message of our collective experience in recovery from addiction. As groups and as a fellowship, we have no opinions on anything but the NA program itself. In our interactions with society, we present only the principles of our program, not our members' personal opinions about other issues.

Anonymity applies not only to our public pronouncements but is the principle underlying the whole of our fellowship's public relations policy. In our public contacts, we base the credibility of our program on NA's effectiveness, not on the personal reputation of any individual member. We seek to attract addicts and gain public goodwill solely by virtue of what we have to offer, not by grandiose promotionalism. Exaggerated claims about NA cannot take the place of the simple, proven validity of our message as the basis of our public relations policy.

Twelfth Tradition anonymity or "namelessness" serves a number of practical functions in our fellowship, each of which has broad spiritual implications. By reminding us that "what's said in this meeting stays in this meeting," our meeting formats help foster an atmosphere in which none of us need to fear public disclosure of what we share in the intimacy of our groups. They also remind us that the message, not the messenger, is what's most important about the sharing that occurs in our meetings.

Twelfth Tradition anonymity also means that, in the final analysis, our personal differences make no difference: In NA, in recovery, we are all equal. It's true that we all come into Narcotics Anonymous with our own personal histories, using patterns, educational and social backgrounds, talents, and shortcomings. But for the purpose of our own recovery, our occupational identity has no bearing on our ability to care for one another in NA. A college degree, a trust fund, illiteracy, poverty—these circumstances that so powerfully affect so many other areas of our lives will neither help nor hinder our chances at recovery. Likewise, they will not aid or impede our efforts to carry the message one addict to another.

We are equal in NA membership. We are all, at last, anonymous "parts of" rather than uniquely "apart from" the NA Fellowship. The anonymity spoken of in our Twelfth Tradition means that, finally, we who have suffered so long from the isolating disease of addiction "belong."

Truly, anonymity is the spiritual foundation of all our traditions. Without it, the unity upon which personal recovery depends would dissolve in a chaos of conflicting personalities. With it, our groups are given a body of guiding principle, our Twelve Traditions, helping them join the personal strengths of their members in a fellowship that supports and nurtures the recovery of us all.

We pray that Narcotics Anonymous never becomes a gray, faceless collection of addicts without personalities. We enjoy the color, the compassion, the initiative, the rough-and-tumble liveliness that arises from the diverse personalities of our members. In fact, our diversity is our strength. We find that the stronger our individual members are, the more strongly united our fellowship becomes. This is a great paradox of NA recovery: In joining together in a commitment to the greater good of Narcotics Anonymous, our own welfare is enhanced beyond measure. In surrendering self-will, humbly placing whatever individual power we may have at the service of the whole, we find an amazing power not only greater than our own but greater than the sum of all its parts. In serving the needs of others selflessly—anonymously—we find our own needs served, in turn, far better than we ever could have imagined. In joining anonymously in a fellowship with other recovering addicts, placing the welfare of the group ahead of our own, our own spiritual growth is enhanced beyond measure, not diminished. This is what Tradition Twelve means when it says that anonymity is the spiritual foundation of all our traditions. So long as we place spiritual principles first, our individual personalities can grow and flourish like never before, ensuring that our fellowship also continues to flourish, strong and free.

Our common welfare depends upon our unity. The only hope we have of maintaining that unity amidst the tremendous diversity we find in Narcotics Anonymous is by the application of certain common principles: those found in the Twelve Traditions. So long as we place the practice of those common principles before the exercise of our individual personalities, all will be well.

INDEX

Index 221

NOTES